SIMON UTTLEY
WITH CONTRIBUTIONS
BY
DR. A. H. CLAIRE

Rebel With A Cause

Sebastian Wolff OSB
Monk   Musician   Pastor

Copyright © 2018 Simon Uttley, Dr A. H. Claire
Editing: Catherine Johnson

Publisher: tredition, Hamburg, Germany

ISBN
Paperback: 978-3-7439-9881-0
Hardcover: 978-3-7439-9882-7
eBook: 978-3-7439-9883-4

Acknowledgements

Chapter 1 – Origins – 1929

Chapter 2 – The Road to Galway

Chapter 3 – The Road to Buckfast

Chapter 4 – Buckfast Abbey c. 1948

Chapter 5 - The Second Vatican Council

Chapter 6 – Ministry

Chapter 7 - A brief commentary on the organ music of Sebastian Wolff and a list of his choral music - By Dr A. H. Claire

Chapter 8 Fellow Travellers – voices of appreciation

Fr Sebastian Wolff

[Sebastian Wolff collection / Buckfast Abbey]

Acknowledgments

This brief look at the long and varied life of one man is not meant as a critical evaluation but, rather, a celebration of how a life, on the face of it so different to most of us, can affect others for the good. I am grateful to all the contributors whose generous comments have helped capture something of our subject. I would particularly like to thank Dr A. H. Claire for his invaluable contributions and encouragement. I am grateful to Liz Keane and the Loughrea choir for their support. Thanks, too, to Cathy Johnson, for her comments and reading. Also, for his support and personal insights, Dr Chris Murray. All errors and omissions remain my own.

Dr Simon Uttley

London, October 2018

AMDG

8

Chapter One - Origins - 1929

The 4th of October 1929 was a day like any other day in Loughrea, some 22 miles East of Galway City, when the young Francis Joseph was born to parents, Karl and Dorothea. The birth was not straightforward and there was a real concern that the baby might not survive, so much so that the Protestant midwife performed a conditional baptism[1] prior to Francis later being baptised again in the local cathedral.

---

[1] A conditional baptism normally takes place if there is uncertainty as to an earlier baptism. Francis, however, would have been re-baptised because of concerns at the time as to the efficacy of the baptism performed.

Fig. 1 Dorothea and Karl

[Courtesy of Sebastian Wolff collection]

Picturesque and bucolic though it may have been, the Galway region had witnessed its own dramas in the years preceding the birth of a boy whose German parentage, itself, was to be one of the many formative strands in the development of the man, the musician and the monk.

Galway city had played a relatively minor role in the upheaval in Ireland from 1916–1923. In 1916, during the Easter Rising, Liam Mellows mobilised the local Irish Volunteers in the area to attack the Royal Irish Constabulary barracks at Oranmore, just outside Galway. However they failed to take it and later surrendered in Athenry. During the Irish War of Independence 1919–21, Galway was the western headquarters for the British Army. Their overwhelming force in the city meant that the local Irish Republican Army could do little against them. The only initiatives were taken by the University battalion of the IRA, who were reprimanded by the local IRA commander who was afraid they would provoke reprisals. This fear was not without justification, as the nearby town of Tuam was sacked on two occasions by the Black and Tans in July and September 1920.

Fig 2 The feared Black and Tans detain a suspected IRA operative [©Military History Now]

In November 1920, a Galway City Catholic priest, Fr. Michael Griffin, was abducted and shot by the British forces. His body was found in a bog in Barna. Galway businessmen launched a boycott against Northern Irish goods from December 1919 onwards in protest against the loyalist attacks on Catholic nationalists in Belfast, a protest that later spread throughout the country.

Before the outbreak of the Irish Civil War (1922–23), in March 1922, Galway saw a tense stand-off between Pro-Treaty and Anti-Treaty troops over who would occupy the military barracks at Renmore. After fighting broke out in July 1922 the city and its military barracks were occupied by troops of the Irish Free State's National Army. Two Free State soldiers and one Anti-Treaty fighter were killed and more wounded before the National Army secured the area. The Republicans burned a number of public buildings in the centre of town before they abandoned Galway.

Into this binary world of, on the one hand, the bucolic - the pastoral - and on the other, significant political upheaval, arguably a defining trope in the Irish narrative, Francis' father had arrived from Germany. And it was another binary – this time the combination of conservative-minded immigrant parentage amid a naturally rebellious landscape- that was, inevitably, to add its own unique ingredient to Francis' worldview.

Francis was the third of a family of nine children, the parents having left Germany in 1927. The Wolff family hailed from the town of Jülich in the Rhineland.

Jülich[2]

A town in the district of Düren, in the federal statre of North Rhine-Westphalia, the town inhabits a border region between the historically competing powers in the Lower Rhine and Mense areas. The town and the Duchy of Jülich played an historic role from the Middle Ages up to the seventeenth century. At the time of the Wolff family's departure the town had a population of approximately 7500, though nowadays it has grown to mearly 40,000 inhabitants.

---

[2] https://www.juelich.de/homepage; Israel, J. [1997] *Conflicts of Empires: Spain, the Low Countries and the Struggle for World Supremacy 1585-1713* London: Hambledon]

Fig. 3 The geography of the Wolff family's hometown

Fig.4 Hexenturm in Julich [courtesy of Shutterstock]

Roman Jülich

Iuliacum, to give it its Roman name, was a small town along the main road from Tongeren, the capital of the Tungri, to Cologne, the capital of Germania Inferior. The town originally belonged to the tribe of the Eburones, and went into decline when Julius Caesar exterminated these people after the insurrection of Ambiorix (winter 54/53).

It appears to have been in c.10 AD that the area was cleared again and used as pasture. This was the district of someone named Julius. This early occupation is logical, because the land is fertile and archaeologists have shown that there were many large farms.

The town was situated east of the crossing of a small river, the Rur, and appears in the Peutinger map, which means that it was a settlement of some significance in the fourth century. This is confirmed by the archaeological record, which shows that at the beginning of the fourth century, *Iuliacum* was fortified with a mighty, fourteen-sided wall. According to the Roman historian Ammianus Marcellinus[3], the castle was still in use in 357, when the area was plundered by a large group of Frankish cavalry. The fort may have been used for an additional half century.

Among the archaeological finds from ancient *Iuliacum* is a fine statue of Jupiter, seated on his throne, made of sandstone. Stylistically, it can be

---

[3] Marcellinus, Ammianus [1986] *The Later Roman Empire AD 354-378 [Hamiliton, W. trans.)* London: Penguin

dated to the first quarter of the third century. Once, it must have graced a column in the court of a villa.

Fortified during the late Roman period, it was taken over by the Franks and grew to be the centre of a county which became the nucleus of a regional power. The counts and dukes of Jülich extended their influence during the Middle Ages and granted Jülich city status in 1234 (Count Wilhelm IV). During battles with the Archbishop of Cologne, Jülich was destroyed in 1239 and again in 1278.

In 1416, the city was granted fiscal independence by Duke Rainald of Jülich-Geldern. Following a fire in 1547, the city was rebuilt as an ideal city in the Renaissance style under the direction of the architect Alessandro Pasqualini. The citadel of Jülich was later visited by the French military engineer Sébastien le Prestre de Vauban and was rated exemplary.

After the ducal family line was extinguished in 1609, the Duchy of Jülich was divided in the War of the Jülich Succession; as part of that war, the fortress at Jülich was occupied by Emperor Rudolph's forces. The siege by Dutch, Brandenburg and Palatine forces led to the surrender and withdrawal of Imperial troops.

Jülich was occupied by the Dutch Republic until 1621-22 when the Spanish took the fortress after a siege of five months. Control of the city later fell to Palatinate-Neuburg, then the Electorate of the Palatinate (1685) and Bavaria (1777).

From 1794 to 1814, Jülich was part of France under the name of *Juliers*. The French added the Napoleonic bridgehead to the fortifications. In 1815, Jülich became a Prussian fortification and district town. The town was subsequently administered within the Prussian Province of Jülich-Cleves-Berg (1815) and then the Rhine Province (1822). The fortification was razed in 1860.

On 16 November 1944 (World War II), 97% of Jülich was destroyed during Allied bombing, since it was considered one of the main obstacles to the occupation of the Rhineland, although the city fortifications, the bridge head and the citadel had long fallen into disuse. The ruined city was subject to heavy fighting for several months until the Allies eventually managed to cross the Rur on 23 February 1945.

World War I

The Wolff's, father Karl and mother, Dorothea, were well known as a musical family. Karl was the eldest of a family of four children. Two brothers, Albert and Heinz-Peter and sister, Kate. Born in 1896, Karl, at the tender age of six, lost his father. At the outbreak of World War I he was pursuing a classical education in Switzerland when his country called on him to take part in one of the defining events in European history.

Karl was to end his military career, but not before participating in the utter carnage which was the Battle of the Somme. This defining experience was captured powerfully in Wilfred Owen's 'Anthem for a Doomed Youth', pertinent for the young men on both sides of the trenches:

What passing-bells for these who die as cattle?

-Only the monstrous anger of the guns.

- Only the stuttering rifles' rapid rattle

-Can patter out their hasty orisons.'

[Owen, 1917; 2013]

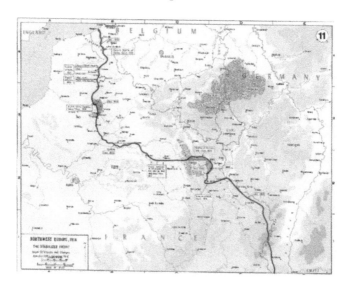

Fig. 5 The Western Front, 1914

The Battle of the Somme

The Battle of the Somme, fought in northern France, was one of the bloodiest of World War One. For five months the British and French armies fought the Germans in a brutal battle of attrition on a 15-mile front. The aims of the battle were to relieve the French Army fighting at Verdun and to weaken the German Army. However, the Allies were unable to break through German lines. In total, there were over one million dead and wounded on all sides. In 141 days, the British had advanced just seven miles and failed to break the German defence. Some historians believe that with a few more weeks of favourable weather the Allies could have broken through German lines. Others argue the Allies never stood a chance. In any case, the British army inflicted heavy losses on the German Army. In March 1917, the Germans made a strategic retreat to the Hindenburg line rather than face the resumption of the Battle of the Somme.

Fig. 6 A German soldier: Battle of the Somme [source: unknown]

'Every German soldier from the highest General to the most lowly private had the feeling that now Germany had lost the great battle' [Oberstleutenant Alfred Bischer][4].

The war was to continue. At the start of 1918, Germany was in a strong position and expected to win the war. Russia had already left the year before, which made Germany even stronger.

Fig.7 "How London hailed the end of war": Front page headline taken from The Daily Mirror on 12 November 1918 [BBC Education]

[4] Simkins, P. [2014:102] *From the Somme to Victory: The British Army's experience on the Western Front 1916-1918* Barnsley, U.K.: The Praetorian Press

Germany launched the 'Michael Offensive' in March 1918, where they pushed Britain far back across the old Somme battlefield. However, their plan for a quick victory failed when Britain and France counter-attacked.

Germany and her allies realised it was no longer possible to win the war. **The Triple Alliance** [Germany, Austria-Hungary and Italy] had been damaged. Some reasons for this included the fact that the Schlieffen Plan had failed in 1914 and the Verdun Offensive had failed in 1916. Germany was now losing the Great Battle in France and the German Navy had gone on strike and refused to carry on fighting. Furthermore, the United States joined the war in April 1917, which gave the Triple Entente [Britain, France and Russia] greater power.

Germany was not strong enough to continue fighting, especially as the USA had joined the war and hundreds of thousands of fresh American soldiers were arriving in France. This added greater military strength to the Triple Entente forces.

The leaders of the German army told the German government to end the fighting. Kaiser Wilhelm, Germany's leader, abdicated on 9 November 1918.

Two days later, Germany signed the armistice and the guns fell silent. People in Britain, France and all of the countries that supported them, celebrated the end of war - a war that had lasted four years and four months. The so-called, and, as it transpired, wrongly-called, *war to end all wars* had come to an end.

However, a proud, deeply cultured and infinitely talented people had been brought to their knees. The bitter taste they were to know for years into the future would have catastrophic consequences for Europe. The Wolff family's destiny would be inextricably linked to the geo-politics which followed.

The Treaty of Versailles

The Versailles Treaty signed at the end of World War I not only lay the moral blame of the conflict on Germany but also forced the Germans to make huge payments to the victors of the war. France and Britain needed these reparations payments in order to pay down their own debts. But they were highly onerous, arguably unjustifiably so, and were deeply unpopular in Germany. Hitler seized on this growing resentment and promised, in the words of Professor Gerd Krumeich, to 'undo this injustice and tear up this treaty and restore Germany to its old greatness'. In fact, the payments demanded were so large that Germany was not able to repay the final instalment of interest until October 3, 2010.[5]

The 1918 Influenza pandemic

As if the young men [and women] of all sides of the hideous conflict had not been through enough – not earned the right for some peace and the consolation of home – it was nature, preying on a ravaged and vulnerable European population, that was to deliver another killer blow. This silent assassin, influenza, killed more people than the great war. Estimates suggest between 20 and 40 million people perished in what was the most devastating

---

[5] http://www.spiegel.de/international/germany/legacy-of-versailles-germany-closes-book-on-world-war-i-with-final-reparations-payment-a-720156.html Viewed 1/4/2010

epidemic in recorded world history, taking more lives in a single year than in the four years of the Black Death bubonic plague of 1347 to 1351. Known as 'Spanish Flu', this represented an international crisis. An estimated 43,000 servicemen were killed by influenza[6]. Thankfully, it did not take Karl, but he did contract it and the results would be significant as we shall see.

Post World War I

At the end of the First World War Francis' father made his way back to Germany where he resumed his career as a musician and his studies at

---

[6] Crosby, A. [1989]. *America's Forgotten Pandemic: The Influenza of 1918,* Cambridge: Cambridge University Press

the Berlin Conservatory. A pianist as well as an organist, Karl studied under a pupil of the great Hans Liszt. Prestigious gigs included the organ of St Hedwig's Catholic church in Berlin.

Fig. 8 St Hedwig's Catholic church, Hinter der Katholischen Kirche 3, Berlin [Courtesy of Shutterstock]

On completion of his studies, as a talented pianist, he gave many concerts and recitals in a country that needed as much cheer as it could get, having been ravaged by war, suffered under incredible economic hardships and been on the receiving end of systematic humiliation from the international community.

The conservatory of Berlin was not the only theatre in which the young Karl was successful, as, in the fullness of time, he also made progress in the theatre of romance. The year 1921 saw him marrying a young Berliner, Dorothea Engelbrecht whose Prussian strength would be, for Francis, something of a mixed blessing growing up. But this strength was not without its benefits as life in postwar Germany was extraordinarily tough and, to make ends meet, Karl was forced to take a very pragmatic approach to his indubitable classical talent by playing the piano in Berlin's bars and restaurants.

However, as the decade progressed, a seismic shift was sweeping across the once-proud Germany. That systematic humiliation on the international stage had not been forgotten. As in so many places, then and now, there can be something alluring about a simple – perhaps overly simplified – message to people who believe themselves wronged. Who is to blame and how can the situation be quickly fixed? A promise to restore pride once more; to identify the villains, root out the trouble makers and offer a glorious, untrammelled future for the *volk*. This seismic shift had a name: National Socialism, and its centre of gravity was none other than Adolf Hitler.

Fig. 9 Hitler speaking with young girls following an address to his supporters 1942 [shutterstock]

Hitler's charism is well documented, as is the effect of the Treaty of Versailles in pushing a proud people into the margins and generating fertile ground for the clear and powerful messages he offered. It is easy, with the benefit of hindsight, to question the support given by intelligent German people to such a despot, but these were different times. People across religious and socio-econimic divides were looking for a future without the benefit of hindsight which the modern reader enjoys. In addition, the attractions of populism, where a charismatic leader tells a people who they should hate, who to fear and who to blame, are phenomena hardly of mere historical interest. Dire economic hardship, a desire for self-respect nationally and internationally, and a fear of communism were just three ingredients playing into the heady cocktail of the *Nationalsozialistische Deutsche Arbeiterpartei*, better known as the Nazi party. Coercion and the fear of recrimination are also effective recruitment sergeants in an atmosphere where normal decency and expectations of behaviour had broken down.

Fig, 10   Good and intelligent people initially succumbed to the spell of National Socialism, including to the Hitler Youth. None other than a 14-year-old Joseph Ratzinger, later Pope Benedict XVI, in full uniform. However, as much as anything it was the fear of condemnation – and compulsion – which drew many young people to 'join up'. [Courtesy www.catholic.org]

Karl's two sons, Karl and Benno, were also initially taken with the message but Karl Junior recounted an incident, shortly before the outbreak of the second World War, when all this changed. Praying in a local Catholic church, Karl and his fellow worshippers witnessed the place of worship being subjected to a vicious and utterly pointless attack by Hitler Youth. Many church furnishings were destroyed and Karl realised immediately the clear and present threat posed by this insidious ideology of hatred. He, too, would make immediate plans to leave the country.

Karl senior, Francis' father, had seen the writing on the wall much earlier. He had realised that Hitler was no saviour leading Germany into a new dawn, liberated from previous military and economic humiliation. Karl saw in Hitler's vindictive obsession with revenge and scapegoating that he was leading Germany into another dark age, yet more chilling than that of the Kaiser. The seventeen million dead from the first conflict – an almost unfathomable number of lost lives, lost dreams - would, almost impossibly, soon be 'upstaged' by the sixty million lost to the second conflict.

The 1918 Flu Pandemic and the Wolff family

However, Nazism was not the only contagion that was to impact the Wolff family. Karl's influenza, contracted during the first conflict, led to a phenomenon very common across Europe at the time. After the 1918 flu pandemic, five million people developed the Parkinson's-like condition *Encephalitis lethargica*. This condition is a disease characterized by high fever, headache, double vision, delayed physical and mental response, and lethargy. In acute cases, patients may enter coma. Patients may also experience abnormal eye movements, upper body weakness, muscular pains, tremors, neck rigidity, and behavioural changes including psychosis. The cause of *encephalitis lethargica* is unknown. Between 1917 and 1928, an epidemic spread throughout the world, but no recurrence of the epidemic has since been reported. Postencephalitic Parkinson's disease may develop after a bout of encephalitis-sometimes as long as a year after the illness.[7] And so it was with Karl, as Sebastian recalls:

[7] National Institute of Neurological Disorders and Stroke https://www.ninds.nih.gov/Disorders/All-Disorders/Encephalitis-Lethargica-Information-Page viewed 1/4/2017

'I remember my father telling me this and that this meant that his hope of a career in music and conducting would be at an end'

The young Francis' relationship with his family was, like so many, multi-facteed and not straightforward, as we will see. But that his parents left an indelible impact is beyond question, an influence, perhaps, steeped in the heady, dangerous formative times endured by his parents. Sebastian describes his parents as 'very strict' and 'strongly influenced by the practice of the Catholic faith in Ireland', hardly an unique phenomenon at the time. Family Rosary took place every morning before the children went to school and Dorothea, a Prussian after all, would brook no disobedience, though with six boys and three girls they would certainly have had their work cut out for them.

Berno, the eldest, Karl, Franz, Wilfried, John Baptist, Joseph, Margarte, Ima and Rose.

Chapter Two - The Road to Galway

Adversity, on occasion, gives way to serendipity and thus was the case for Karl and his family when he became aware of musician posts available in a range of Irish ecclesiastical settings. Posts which could offer a viable standard of living for Dorothea and the children away from the volatility, and downright danger of Germany. And the Wolffs were by no means unique in looking abroad for new opportunities.

Germany in the last hundred years or so has rarely been a country to leak talent in the form of emigration. Its high standard of living, education and culture has made it a magnet to others. Whether in the fields of music, technology, good government or innovation, Germany has so long been a byword for quality. However, the 1920s was an exception. As Kirk comments:

'The first world war resulted in a brief revival of emigration from Germany... The loss of territory and the economic hardships ... set in motion a new wave of emigration which never matched the flood of the 1850s and the 1880s but nevertheless supplied some half million emigrants in the 1920s'[8]

No wonder then that the offer, in 1928, of the post of Cathedral organist in Loughrea, Galway,

---

[8] Kirk, D. [1946:89]. *Europe's Population in the Interwar Years. Vol. 3* London & New York : Gordon & Breach

offered Karl an opportunity to continue his passion for music and provide a fresh opportunity for his young family.

Continental Musicians in Ireland

Very much on Karl's radar were some of the continental organists who had made Ireland their home and would go on to contribute significantly to the cultural life of the country. [9] Sebastian recollects the following as examples.

---

[9] Deacy, M.R. [2005:121] 'Continental Organists and Catholic Church Music in Ireland, 1860-1960' M. Litt Dissertation *National University of Ireland, Maynooth*

Ernest de Regge

De Regge arrived in Ennis, Co. Clare, in 1923, and remained until his death in 1958. De Regge was a classmate and the two were firm friends. As well as being organist and choir director in the cathedral, de Regge taught chant and music in St Flannan's College, Ennis. In the 1930s, he was very active in the Gregorian revival in the county and was instrumental in establishing a society called the 'Association of St Gregory' for the promotion of church music in the diocese

Aloys Fleischmann

One of the most important and influential German organists in Ireland at the time was Aloys Fleischmann (1880-1964). Fleischmann, who came to Cork in 1906, had an immense influence on the practice and development of sacred music in the city of Cork over a fifty-year period. He was a graduate of the Royal Academy of Music in Munich and after Fleischmann graduated with great distinction in his final exams, he took up a post as organist in his hometown of Dachau. In 1906, Fleischmann married Tily Swertz, whom he had met as a student in Munich. She was an accomplished pianist and daughter of Cork cathedral organist, Conrad Swertz. Tily Swertz brought her new husband to Cork to replace her father as cathedral organist in 1906. As organist in St Mary's Cathedral, Cork, Aloys Fleischm adhered strictly to the decrees of Motu Proprio and continued to do so until the early 1960s. According to comments by made by his son in 1957, Fleischmann made sweeping changes to sacred music practice in the city following the publication of Motu Proprio[10]. His efforts including the substitution of boys' for women's voices and the abandonment of the Masses of Mozart, Haydn and Gounod, at first met with considerable opposition. He studied in the Munich Conservatoire and taught there between the years 1859-1901 as court conductor, organist and composer. A prolific composer of operas, symphonies, chamber music, and choral works, he is remembered almost exclusively for his elaborate and challenging organ compositions which included two

---

[10] The *Motu Proprio* document on sacred music issued on the feast of St Cecilia, 22 November 1903 by Pius X was seen as the conclusion of the reform of church music which had been ongoing since the mid-nineteenth century. The proclamation was the climax of previous work done by Pius X on music legislation. The document clearly laid down the regulations of the catholic church as regards the use of sacred music in the liturgy.

concertos, twenty sonatas, twenty-two trios, twelve *Meditations* and thirty-six other solo pieces.

Aloys Fleishmann was one of the pupils of this distinguished musician which included Engelbert Humperdinck, Ermanno Wolf-Ferrari, Bela Bartók, and Zoltán Kodaly. Fleischmann was interned during the First World War and after an initial period of custody in a camp in Co. Meath, was sent to the Isle of Man. On the Isle of Man, Fleischmann established a choir and orchestra from amongst his fellow German residents in the camp. The bishop of Cork allowed Fleischmann's wife, Tily, to take over the training of the choir during Aloy's absence.

Tily Swertz-Fleischmann

Bom in Cork in 1883, Tily was a talented pianist. She was sent by her father, Conrad Swertz, to study piano at the Royal Academy of Music in Munich from 1901 to 1906, where she took master classes with Munich virtuoso and conductor, Bernard Stavenhagen, who was the last pupil of Franz Listz. Before returning to Cork, Tily Fleischmann gave several recitals in Munich, and played under the baton of the famous Austrian conductor Felix Mottl (1856-1911). She founded the Listz tradition of piano playing in Ireland and taught at the Cork School of Music. She was also the first pianist from Ireland to give a BBC radio broadcast in 1929. Considering that women were banned from choirs following the *Motu Proprio* document in 1903, this was a courageous as well as a kind gesture on the part of the bishop.

Fleischmann was not allowed to return to Cork after the war in 1918. Instead, he was returned to Germany where he remained for another two years before being permitted to return to Cork. Fleischmann established a fine choir of about fifty boys and forty men who sang primarily Gregorian chant and the sixteenth-century repertoire. He also introduced modern sacred compositions by German composers such as Goller (a fellow student in Munich), and Rheinberger.

Jean Thauet gives way to Karl Wolff

Deacy notes that often foreign organists themselves, on their return trips, would have been influential in bringing other organists to Ireland. This may have been the case with Gustav Haan, a brother of Alphonse, who came to Carlow cathedral in 1892. German organists in Ireland often contacted colleagues in Germany about vacancies in Irish churches and cathedrals which ensured the continuation of a tradition that had became established by the turn of the twentieth century. Cities and towns such as Cork, Longford and Loughrea boasted several German organists possibly indicating that this was the case.

'This was the case in Loughrea cathedral, Co. Galway. The organist Jean Thauet told his colleague Karl Wolff in Germany about the position that he was vacating in 1927, and Wolff came to Ireland in the same year to take up the appointment.'[11]

---

[11] Deacy *op. cit. footnote* 44

She goes on to give a fitting tribute to Karl's contribution between 1927 and 1980:

'Wolff did much to improve sacred and secular music conditions in Loughrea. For a town of only 2,000 inhabitants in the 1930s, Loughrea boasted, under Wolff's direction, a substantial four-part cathedral choir capable of singing Gregorian chant and sixteenth-century polyphony. Wolff was also a prolific sacred music composer and the choir in Loughrea regularly sang his compositions. He also taught music in Garbally, the diocesan boys' college in Ballinasloe, where he directed an annual student operetta. He taught piano, organ and trained a brass band in the town. He wrote and scored music for many plays in Loughrea throughout the 1930s which proved very successful, with performances attracting audiences from many parts of Galway'[12]

Karl made his way to Loughrea alone and then, in 1928, was joined by Dorothea. Benno and Karl stayed in school in Germany until 1939. Benno was in Junior Seminary in Oberbach, Bavaria, until its closure that year. In scenes resembling a Hollywood movie, the two older brothers managed to board the last ship out of the country prior to the gates being closed to exit.

---

[12] Deacy *op. cit.* footnote 128

Loughrea

Loughrea, or *Baile Locha Riach*, (meaning "town of the grey lake") is a town in County Galway lying to the north of a range of wooded hills, the Slieve Aughty Mountains, and the lake from which it takes its name. The town is famous for its cathedral, St Brendan's, designed by William Byrne, begun in 1897 and completed in 1902. As the principal church of the Diocese of Clonterf, like the institutional Church into which Francis was born and would subsequently commit his life, St Brendan's dominated the town's skyline. Described as the 'jewel of the Celtic revival', the architecture owed much to 'The International Arts & Crafts Movement' of the late 19th century, that sought to reunite the artist and the craftsman. An edifice, then, born out of a reaction to the mass

me – not least as she was often in another room when she proffered her opinions'

Prior to the inevitable breaking of the voice, Francis also offered a very serviceable choral contribution, able to hit a top C. For this reason he was, understandably, encouraged to sing in the Cathedral choir.

But it was not all pianos and organs – the National School also provided him with the opportunity to learn the bagpipes, such that Francis later joined a local pipe band. 'I became proficient in the pipes' he said 'and had a certain love for the Irish pipes'.

It was at College in Limerick, however, as he scribbled down melodies and harmony, that Francis took a turn towards the musical genre which would characterise his life's work. Benefitting, as is so often the case, from an inspirational teacher whose dexterity on the keyboard, powering out, *inter alia*, Beethoven sonatas, proved inspirational to the young man from Loughrea, Francis now added Mozart and Haydn to his list of much-loved composers. Later, when at home, Francis revelled in the music of Chopin and the Russian composers.

However, it was not all high-powered classics. Francis' father, possibly drawing on that sense of practicality and pragmatism that wartime and post-war Germany had taught him, made use of his talents to play piano at a range of gigs in the town, including Latin American pieces which Francis found 'quite exciting'. Many years later, after his ordination in 1955, Francis would draw on this when he was asked to write music for the piano and launched into tango and similar genres. This blending was essential to develop an openness and creativity which would prove foundational.

Francis' brother Benno, joined an Irish Junior seminary run by the Society of African Missions, better known as the SMA Fathers, just outside of Castlebar, Co. Mayo. Sebastian recalls a seminal event that reflects the relative insularity of his life in rural Galway - going to visit his brother with his father:

'My father took me – a small young boy – on the back of his motorbike. It was my first trip outside Co. Galway. '

Brother Karl, on the other hand, was schooled in Loughrea where, as a bright young man, he quickly picked up the Irish language – rather important given this was the language through which lessons were taught. The linguistic 'richness' of the Wolff family's new reality was impressive: Irish spoken at school, German at home and English in the street! The migrant experience – and, in particular, the children of migrants - for millenia, has always seen the migrant family having to make do and get on with things, to blend in and to learn quickly. So often migrant families are desperate to contribute to their new home, and new homeland, as their children grow up with multiple, though, hopefully, complementary, identities. This invariably gives the migrant family an energy and drive which is unusually strong and remains formative. An energy and a positivity which, as we know in our own time, can be lost on the small-minded and easily-threatened. Though the son of migrants rather than a migrant himself, the later Fr Sebastian's strength as a person and, later, as a monk and musician may well partly reflect this expereince.

As Francis began to consider his vocation, the *De La Salles* were not the only Congregation to share their charism with this talented young man. The Redemptorist order, too, played a brief role in his childhood: brief but significant.

St Clement's College, founded in 1884 at a time when every religious order and congregation worth their salt wanted a guaranteed production line to fill the ranks, was, for a time, both the Juniorate [a form of junior seminary] and the school of choice as Francis discerned whether a vocation to the apostolic life of a Redemptorist was for him.

Not so, it transpired, as the Redemptorists did not see him as having a vocation to their particular way of life and so he returned to Loughrea to complete his secondary education. It was at this time that the prayers of St Benedict overtook those of St Alphonsus Ligouri and, through a chance glance at a leaflet given to him by a local Loughrea publican entitled 'Buckfast Abbey', Francis first became aware of [to him] an obscure and unknown place across the Irish sea. A place that would come to be his home for the next sixty years. Buckfast Abbey in South Devon.

Chapter Three – The Road to Buckfast

While the author or typsetter of that now long-lost pamphlet may, from their celestial vantage point, rightly take some credit for the early fostering of this fledgling vocation to the Benedictine religious life, it was, for Francis, as much as anything else, the fact that this religious house lay beyond Erin's shores that attracted him. As for so many native-born Irishmen before him and since, he saw a future beyond the fields and turf of Loughrea and it was this, together with his knowledge that the Benedictines had a long tradition in music and the sung Divine Office [13] that led him to

---

[13] The Divine Office is the prayer of the Church said at various times each day, beginning with Matins and ending with Night prayer, or Compline. Certain variations are authorized for specific monastic communities.

contact the Novice Master, and later Abbot, of Buckfast Abbey, one Dom Placid Hooper OSB.

Dom Placid Hooper OSB

Placid Hooper [14] would subsequently become the fourth abbot of the restored Buckfast Abbey in Devon, and the first Englishman to hold this position as father and superior of the house. He set the monastery on its course from a German community, belonging to an Italian grouping of Abbeys, to, instead, an English Benedictine community which is what it remains to this day.

---

[14] *The Independent 28th December 1995*

Father Placid was born Thomas Hooper, in 1911, into a family of Taunton grocers. He was educated at Huish's Grammar School in Taunton and, in 1929, joined the community at Buckfast, where he was given the name of Placid. He made his profession as a monk the following year and, after the prescribed theological studies, was ordained priest in 1935. As the intricate ceremonial of liturgical functions required dedicated specialists, Father Placid, who had been keenly interested in the liturgy since he was a junior monk, was appointed Master of Ceremonies.

In the Second World War Placid Hooper was one of four English members of the community allowed to offer their services as Chaplains to the Armed Forces. He was called up in 1939 and attached to a medical unit, seeing distinguished service in France and Belgium (escaping via Dunkirk), then with the Eighth Army in the Middle East, Italy, Greece and Austria.

On his return to Buckfast in 1945 he was appointed Novice Master, an experienced monk whose task it is to train the aspirants to the monastic life according to the Benedictine Rule as lived at Buckfast. In addition, the novitiate is also a time of discernment as the monk is not, at this point, solemnly professed for life. With his interest in the liturgy and his encyclopaedic knowledge of Buckfast's history, Fr Placid was well equipped for such a role. It was he who would meet Francis at the station and kick-start [in every way] the young Irishman's vocation.

Music at Buckfast

Music and Buckfast have gone hand in hand for many years. The atmospheric surroundings of the Abbey Church, the magnificent organ, now replaced in the twenty-first century with a powerful new instrument, the sense of timelesness and transcendence all add to the experience of live music. In 2018, for example, as the monastery reconised 1000 years since monasticism first took root next to the Dart, the Abbey Church provided a feast of music. But what about during the time that Sebastian was a young monk and the year Fr Placid was made Abbot? Looking at the *Radio Times* BBC TV listings for Sunday 20th October 1957, for example, we see that Buckfast was very much on the musical radar.

From Buckfast Abbey, Devon.

Celebrant, Dom Leo Smith O.S.B, the Prior

Preacher, The Rt. Rev. Placid Hooper O.S.B., the Abbot

of Buckfast

The action of the Mass described by Father Agnellus

Andrew O.F.M.

The Bells

The Asperges

Introit; Kyrie; Gloria Collect

Lesson: from Ephesians 4 Gradual

Gospel: St. Matthew 22 Sermon

Credo No. 1

Offertory

Preface; Sanctus

The Consecration

Benedictus; Pater Noster;

Agnus Dei

The Communion

Post Communion

The Blessing

The Last Gospel: St. John 1

Choirmaster, Dom Charles Norris O.S.B.

Organist, Dom Gregory Burke O.S.B.

Master of the Ringing, Dom Oswald Mowan
O.S.B.

The Proper of the Mass is from the 19th Sunday
after Pentecost; the Common of the Mass from
Alissa: Orbis Factor.

The English Benedictine Congregation

Dom[15] Placid was elected Abbot in 1957 and, in the same year, he realised that, with a community now almost entirely English, it would be easier if the administrative links with the Continent were broken in favour of closer links with the other Benedictine monasteries in England, such as Downside (the senior house) in Somerset, Ampleforth in North Yorkshire and Douai in Berkshire. Therefore, in 1960, Buckfast was officially transferred to the English Benedictine Congregation.

At the time of writing there are ten UK and three overseas Houses within the English Benedictine Congregation [EBC]. Although the EBC

---

[15] 'Dom', derived from 'Dominus' – a prefix used in most monastic communities which, on its own, connotes neither ordained, nor non-ordained, status.

claims technical canonical continuity with the congregation erected by the Holy See in 1216, that earlier English Congregation was destroyed at the Dissolution of the Monasteries in 1535-40. The present English Congregation was revived and restored by Rome in 1607-33 when numbers of Englishmen and Welshmen had become monks in continental European monasteries and were coming to England as missioners.

Every four years the General Chapter of the EBC elects an Abbot President from among the Ruling Abbots with jurisdiction, and those who have been Ruling Abbots. He is assisted by a number of officials. Periodically he undertakes a Visitation of the individual Houses. The purpose of the Visitation is the preservation, strengthening and renewal of the religious life, including the laws of the Church and the Constitutions of the congregation. The President may require by Acts of Visitation, that particular points in the Rule of St Benedict[16], the Constitutions and the law of the Church be observed.

Francis prepares to become Dom Sebastian

In the contemporary world of religious vocations, however counter-cultural, even alien to many, there is now a recognition that the process of discerning a vocation to a vowed life should be slow, measured, systematic and subject to the checks and balances associated with such a significant step. So one might expect a young aspirant from rural Ireland, who had never left the region

---

[16] The book of precepts written by St Benedict of Nursia [c. AD 480-550] for monks [and nuns] living communally under the authority of an abbot.

let alone the country, to be encouraged, over a period of time, to gently discern his or her vocation. Completing some higher academic or vocational study might also give the aspirant time to mature. Certainly a few visits of a few days – perhaps a week or more – would obviously be required if the young man was considering making a vow of Stability such that this one place would be his home for the rest of his life. Meetings, reference requests, in some places psychometric tests and profiling to evaluate the aspirant's mindset would all seem reasonable and sensible in the modern world. But young Francis was not growing up in the twenty-first century, and, as L.P Hartley famously said, *'The past is a foreign country; they do things differently there'*. And so they did!

An exchange of letters between the West of Ireland and South Devon and arrangements were concluded – in a fortnight! Francis would leave his home to go to a place he had never visited and would, figuratively, not see the light of day for the subsequent four years. This was monastic life before the Second Vatican Council. Call it inhumane on occasion, call it radical. What is certain is that it was uncompromising; definitive.

On the 11th November 1948 Francis's train pulled out of the station bound for Dublin – itself no mean trial in a period where Irish transportation still retained much of the dubious charm depicted in John Ford's film, *The Quiet Man*. Francis's elder brother, by now a professed son of Jean-Baptiste de La Salle[17] having already entered that Congregation, asked his younger brother to spend the night at the Congregation's house in Dublin. The following morning Francis took the train from Dublin to Wexford and from there, ostensibly a trivial matter of a crossing to Fishguard.

The night of the 12th November Francis set sail. He left an Ireland where the President was Seán T. O'Kelly and the Taoiseach, until February that year, had been Éamon de Valera before his

---

[17] The Brothers of the Christian Schools (also known as the Christian Brothers, the Lasallian Brothers, the French Christian Brothers, or the De La Salle Brothers; French: *Frères des écoles chrétiennes*; Latin: *Fratres Scholarum Christianarum*) is a Roman Catholic religious teaching congregation, founded in France by Jean-Baptiste de La Salle (1651–1719), and now based in Rome.

Fianna Fail party had lost to John A. Costello's Fine Gael. De Valera, however controversial, held an iconic position in the rebel tradition of the island of Ireland. As a commander in the 1916 Easter Rising, De Valera was a political leader in the War of Independence and of the anti-Treaty opposition in the ensuing Irish Civil War (1922–1923). His political life epitomised the ideal formed from a juxtaposition of the pastoral – the bucolic, profoundly Catholic conservatism which he espoused – with a readiness to play a full part in what the British State deemed *terrorist acts*. Again, the respectable, deeply cultured rebel – to others a terrorist - at the heart of the Irish story.

Elsewhere rationing had just ended in Dublin after six years. Ireland, too, had suffered notwithstanding the sometimes difficult issue [to some] of its neutrality during World War II. It would be two more years before John Ford would begin to shoot *The Quiet Man* and give Galway and Mayo another touristic shot in the arm and the body of W. B. Yeats was re-buried at Drumcliffe, County Sligo, 'Under bare Ben Bulben's head'. Finally, propitious or otherwise to Francis' impending voyage, a 36-foot shark had been spotted off the coast of County Donegal. Scary, but no match for a Benedictine Novice Master.

But what of Francis' destination: Britain and the Catholic Church in the late 1940s?

George VI reigned over an empire whose fortunes were on the turn. Clem Atlee was Prime Minister of a bombed out and financially broke country where the post-war celebrations had given way to the post-war hangover of rationing and significant economic hardship. After World War II, the British economy had, again, lost huge amounts of absolute wealth. Its economy was driven entirely by the needs of war and took some time to be reorganised for peaceful production. The winter of 1946–1947 had proven to be very harsh, curtailing production and leading to shortages of coal, which again affected the economy. The loss of the Empire and the material losses incurred through two world wars had affected the basis of Britain's economy. Indeed, Prime Minister Atlee was overseeing the process of Indian independence, and Francis would soon be boarding a British rail train, the railway network having been nationalised earlier that year.

The London Co-operative Society had opened Britain's first supermarket, in Manor Park, London. The Australian cricket team had come to England and returned home, having not lost a match and Manchester United had defeated Blackpool 4–2 in the FA Cup final at Wembley Stadium, to claim their first major trophy for 37 years. Just four days before Francis boarded the boat to Wales, Princess Elizabeth had given birth to the future prince Charles. Britain was rationed and many urban bomb sites were yet to be cleared.

In Rome, Eugenio Maria Giuseppe Giovanni Pacelli, better known as Pope Pius XII, reigned over a Church still reeling from war. Pius XII explained the Catholic faith in 41 encyclicals and almost 1000 messages and speeches during his long pontificate. *Mediator Dei* clarified membership and participation in the Church. The encyclical *Divino afflante Spiritu* opened the doors for biblical research. His magisterium was far larger and is difficult to summarize. In numerous speeches Catholic teaching is related to various aspects of life, education, medicine, politics, war and peace, the life of saints, Mary, the Mother of God, things eternal and contemporary. Theologically, Pius XII specified the nature of the teaching authority of the Church. He also gave a new freedom to engage in theological investigations. During the war, *Time* magazine credited Pius XII and the Catholic Church for "fighting totalitarianism more knowingly, devoutly and authoritatively, and for a longer time, than any other organised power."

On 1 November 1950, Pius XII defined the dogma of the Assumption of Mary, namely that she, "having completed the course of her earthly life, was assumed body and soul into heavenly glory." The dogma was preceded by the 1946 encyclical *Deiparae Virginis Mariae*, which requested all Catholic bishops to express their opinion on a possible dogmatization. On 8 September 1953, the encyclical *Fulgens corona* announced a Marian year for 1954, the centennial of the Dogma of the Immaculate Conception. In the encyclical *Ad caeli reginam* he promulgated the Queenship of Mary feast. At Buckfast, too, the devotion to our Lady of Buckfast, with her statue in its commanding niche high above the altar, would have been a detail not lost on the young Francis.

Figure 12 Pope Pius X [courtesy: Rorate Coeli]

But the propsect of contemplating the finer points of the Abbey church's iconography was probably not on the mind of Francis who, enduring gale-force winds in a vessel without stabilisers on a crossing that tested the metal of even the most resilient of mariners, left him with thirty-six deplorable hours of sea sickness.

Nevertheless, with youth on his side, his appetite remained intact, even if he barely had enough money to buy a drink and a sandwich. Jaded but focussed, he made his way to Bristol to catch the train to the South Devon market town of Newton Abbot, itself named after the 'New Town of the Abbots' of Torre Abbey, the twelfth century monastery in Torquay built by the Premonstratensian Canons.

On his arrival at the Abbey, Francis was shown to what would be his quarters for the next four years – the Novitiate - where the aspirant discerns his vocation while living the life of a monk. As Francis looked out from his cell window, a busker passed by and, in a moment worthy of the great John Ford himself, this down-at-heel troubadour placed his trumpet to his lips and played the doleful melody that is guaranteed to bring a tear to the eye of every Irish *ex pat* wherever they find themselves. What else but '*Galway Bay.*'?

Chapter Four - Buckfast Abbey c. 1948

Figure 13 Buckfast Abbey Church [Shutterstock]

To say that the Novice Master of a religious order or congregation plays a key role in the life of an aspiring 'Religious' would be an understatement. The Novice Master, together with the other senior members of the monastic community [including the Abbot and the Prior] are hugely influential, and none more so than Dom Placid, whose governance of what might nowadays be called the 'novice experience' was absolute. But more of the Novitiate anon. What *was* this post-war monastic life to which Francis entered?

Buckfast first became home to an Abbey in 1018. The Abbey was believed to be founded by either Aethelweard (Aylward), Earldorman of Devon [Beattie, 1997; Emery, 2006] or King Cnut. This first monastery was "small and unprosperous", and it is unknown where exactly it was located, and its existence was precarious especially after the Norman Conquest [18]. The first Benedic-

---

[18] http://www.pastscape.org.uk/hob.aspx?hob_id=1266782

tine Abbey was followed by a Savignac (later Cistercian) Abbey constructed on the site of the current Abbey in 1134. In 1134 or 1136, the Abbey was established in its current position; King Stephen having granted Buckfast to the French Abbot of Savigny. This second Abbey was home to Savignac monks. In 1147 the Savignac congregation merged with the Cistercian, and the Abbey thereby became a Cistercian monastery. Following the conversion to the Cistercian Congregation, the Abbey was rebuilt in stone. Limited excavation work undertaken in 1882 revealed that the monastery was built to the standard plan for Cistercian monasteries.

At the time of the Dissolution of the Monasteries, the last Abbot, Gabriel Donne (d.1558), despite the solemn oaths he had taken, on 25 February 1539, together with nine others of his religious community, surrendered his Abbey into the hands of Sir William Petre, as agent for King Henry VIII. On 26 April 1539 he was rewarded with a large annual pension of £120 which he enjoyed until his death. The other monks, who all co-signed the deed of surrender, also received smaller pensions. The site of the Abbey was granted by the King to Sir Thomas Dennis (c.1477-1561) of Holcombe Burnell. in Devon, who had married Donne's sister Elizabeth and was Chamberlain of the Household to Cardinal Wolsey.

Following dissolution, the Abbey site and its lands were granted by the crown to Sir Thomas Denys (c.1477-1561) of Holcombe Burnell, near Exeter, who stripped the buildings and "reduced them to ruins". The Abbey site was subsequently used as a stone quarry.

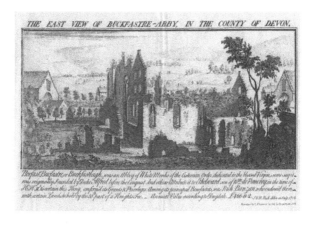

Figure 14 The Abbey in ruins [fragment: source Sebastian Wolff collection]

In 1882 the site was purchased by a group of French Benedictine monks, who refounded a monastery on the site, dedicated to the Mother of God, Saint Mary. New monastic buildings and a temporary church were constructed incorporating the existing Gothic house. Work on a new Abbey church, which was constructed mostly on the footprint of the former Cistercian Abbey, started in 1907. The church was consecrated in 1932 but not completed until 1938.

Buckfast was formally reinstated as an Abbey in 1902, and the first abbot of the new institution, Boniface Natter, was blessed in 1903.

By the 16th century, the Abbey was in decline. Only 22 new monks were ordained between 1500 and 1539, and at the time of the Abbey's dissolution, there were only 10 monks in residence.

In 1800, the site was purchased by local mill owner, Samuel Berry. Berry had the ruins demolished, constructing a Gothic style "castellated Tudor" mansion house, and a wool mill on the site in 1806. The Gothic house was constructed on the site of the Abbey's former west cloister. The only pieces of the former Abbey to escape demolition were some of the outer buildings - which were retained as farm buildings - and a tower from the former abbot's lodgings, the only part which remains to this day.

In 1872 the site came into the possession of Dr. James Gale. Dr. Gale chose to sell the site in 1882 and, wishing to offer it for religious use, advertised the estate as "a grand acquisition which could be restored to its original purpose".

In 1882 the whole site was purchased by French Benedictine monks, who had been exiled from the Abbaye Sainte-Marie de la Pierre-qui-Vire in 1880. On 28 October 1882, six Benedictine monks arrived at Buckfast having been exiled from France. The land had been leased by monks from the St. Augustine's Priory in Ramsgate and it was later bought for £4,700.

Most of Samuel Berry's house was remodel-led and incorporated into new claustral ranges which were built in 1882. A temporary church was constructed to the south of these new buildings, with the current Abbey church constructed between 1906 and 1938, mostly on the footprint of the Cistercian Abbey. The new Abbey church was built in the "Norman Transitional and Early English" styles, to the designs of architect, Frederick Arthur Walters. There were never more than six monks working on the project at any one time, although the whole community had repaired the ancient foundations up to ground level. Construction methods were primitive: wooden scaffolding was held together by ropes and no safety protection was worn by the monks. One monk fell 50 feet but survived; and three monks fell off a hoist without serious injury in 1931. Construction continued throughout the war; some of the monks were of

German nationality, but were not sent to an internment camp on condition that they remained confined to the Abbey grounds. Indeed, in later years, when Francis had become Fr Sebastian, he drew on his knowledge of the German language to act as confessor with the German-speaking members of the community, including the world-famous bee expert, Karl Kehrle OBE, better known by his name in religion, Brother Adam.

In terms of the formal statis of the monastery, Buckfast was formally reinstated as an Abbey in 1902, and Boniface Natter - who died at sea in 1906, when the SS *Sirio* was shipwrecked - was blessed as the new abbot on 24 February 1903. His travelling companion Anscar Vonier became the next abbot and pledged to fulfil Natter's dying wish, namely to rebuild the Abbey.

The Abbey church was consecrated on 25 August 1932, but the building was not finished for several years: the last stone was laid in late 1937, merely 11 years prior to Francis's arrival and final works completed the following year.

Buckfast Abbey in 1948[19]

Shortly prior to Sebastian's arrival at Buckfast, the new Mosaic payment had been laid onto the lantern. The memorial plaque of Abbott Anscar, described in the Buckfast Abbey Chronicle for spring of 1948 as "the prime mover of the Abbey's restoration"[20] had been completed thanks to the artistry of Bennie Elkan. The Abbott was

---

[19] 'The Buckfast Abbey Chronicle' – Spring 1948 Buckfast Abbey Henceforth BAC
[20] *ibid. 1*

clearly wrestling with issues which resonate today. While he acknowledged that it is an axiom of Benedictine tradition that nothing is too precious for God's service, at the same time he was aware that the community was living through a time of austerity in the immediate post-war period. However, he was comfortable that, given the donor's express wish for the beautification of the Abbey, it was right and proper that this was what the money was spent on, notwithstanding the importance of supporting the needy.

'The need for beautiful things is all the greater in time when necessity wears down the spirit of man' [21]

---

[21] *ibid. 2*

The Abbott congratulated Brother Adam, Buck-fast's famous beekeeper, for his exceptional skill and knowledge. Brother Adam had been appointed a member of a government advisory committee liaising between beekeepers and the Ministry of Agriculture. No small achievement for a monk, and a German monk at that! This was to ensure that the strains of bees throughout the country could be improved. One of the four strains chosen for this experiment was the one that brother Adam had perfected in the apiaries of Buckfast over many years.

Fig.15 Brother Adam [formerly Karl Kehrle] OBE 1898– 1996 [Sebastian Wolff collection]

He was unsurpassed as a breeder of bees. He talked to them, he stroked them. He brought to the hives a calmness that, according to those who saw him at work, the sensitive bees responded to [22]

Fr Jerome Gladman, later to become Sub Prior and himself a musician, had, together with another monk, volunteered with the Abbot's permission, to go to East Africa to assist German Benedictines. As well as departures there was a welcome to newcomers to the ranks of the community including a new postulant, Vincent Arnold, later Dom Gabriel Arnold who, together with Sebastian, was to become one of the elder statesmen of the

---

[22] Colquohoun, K., Wroe, A. [2008:185] *The Economist Book of Obituaries*. London: Profile Books

twenty-first   century   monastic   community.

The death was announced of Herr Bernhard Witte, described as 'the goldsmith of Aachen'[23] who had contributed to several iconic features of the contemporary monastery: the high altar, the baptismal font and Corona, the stations of the cross,   the   choir   lectern   and   chalices. Elsewhere across the Benedictine world, the celebration had taken place to mark the 14th century of the death of Saint Benedict, on 18 September 1947. Some 100 Benedictine Abbotts were present on this occasion where the Holy Father, Pope Pius XII,   delivered   his   Latin   address.

---

[23] BAC, 5

Very much resonant with the immediate post-war period - though with echoes of today - the address was warm in its adulation of Saint Benedict, yet withering in its condemnation of the contemporary decline in faith: 'Europe has turned away from the Royal Road of Saint Benedict'[24].

Dom Charles Norris, the great glass artist of the Abbey, discussed the critical reception of the bronze memorial to Abbot Anscar Vonier, the founding Abbot of the contemporary monastery.

---

[24] ibid. 9

Fig. 16 Abbot Anscar Vonier, 1875-1938
[Buckfast Abbey]

He noticed that, at the Royal Academy, and at Buckfast it was admired as "a portrayal of the Abbot's maturity -large, determined, triumphant." At the same time for others, recognising the subjectivity in all art, it was "thought to be dark, sinister and repellent."

Its subject was no small figure in inter-war theology. *Author of 'A Key to the Doctrine of the Eucharist',* Vonier's work was later described by Aidan Nichols as 'a classic example of the twentieth century's best eucharistic theology'.[25]

Many years later, another Abbot, Leo Smith, spoke generously of the bronze – and its subject:

There the Abbot, a figure of no small stature, is depicted as offering his life's work to Our Lady to whom the Abbey is dedicated. There is an epic quality about the story developed in the scroll of the plaque...'

[25] Nichols, A. [1991 :102] *The Holy Eucharist: From The New Testament to Pope John Paul II.* Eugene, OR : Wipf & Stock

Fig.17 The Vonier Memorial Plaque, Buckfast Abbey

[Photograph: Simon Uttley]

He goes on 'The young monk saved from a shipwreck in which his abbot perished; his own election as abbot; the decision to rebuild the Abbey church; the first load of stone from the quarry delivered in a borrowed horse and cart; the labour of building with no modern equipment, and the final touch, his acclaim of the finished work with the skeleton of death calling him to his reward'[26]

Thus a key element in the unique narrative of Buckfast Abbey was to find its place in the Abbey Church to remind all of the drama and the sacrifice that lay at the foundation of the modern community.

---

[26] Smith, Dom Leo, 'The Life and Work of Abbot Anscar Vonier' Dom Leo Smith 'English Benedictine Congregation History Commission' (1996) 1-17 p. 1 http://www.monlib.org.uk/papers/ebch/1996smith.pdf viewed 3/3/17

'I was more attracted to religious life than to the priesthood. The question of deciding to go on to study for the priesthood only came to me when I had already come to Buckfast'

\- Sebastian Wolff

Fig. 18 A striking young Dom Sebastian

[courtesy: Sebastian Wolff collection]

Away from Vonier, Dom Charles goes on to describe the pavements and floorings of the Abbey Church which, some seventy-five years later, would be beautifully restored under Abbot David Charlesworth and are visible in the modern-day Abbey church. Dom Stephan discusses the virtues of the Catholic family, concluding that 'To provide saints for heaven is a greater achievement than to produce men and women of genius'.[27]

This same year a few religious books received the honour of a review in the Buckfast Abbey Chronicle. Dom Aelred Graham's 'The History of Catholicism' 'will not disappoint us', as 'of lasting profit for the spiritual life'[28]. S.M Shaw's 'Salt of the Earth' has for its purpose 'to help the young

---

[27] BAC, 44
[28] ibid. 44-45

priest to translate into the realm of living fact the doctrines of ascetical theology learned in the seminary' so as to teach him to 'focus both his work and his prayer on Christ'.[29]

Beyond theology, the impact of continental psychology was felt in the fascinating 'Personal Mental Hygiene', penned by Dom Thomas Verner Moore which gave the reader an insight into the clinical application of the works of, among others, Jung, Freud and Adler. Finally, 'The Spell of the Honey Bee' by a certain W.E. Lelsey received a review by none other than Brother Adam. However much Adam was, and in many ways remained in outlook, a pre-Vatican II Lay Brother, his expertise placed him in a different space than many of his contemporaries.

---

[29] ibid. 47

Dom Sebastian – the young monk and musician

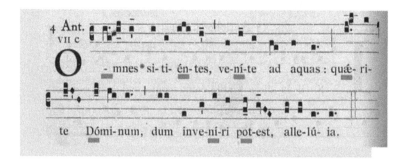

Figure 19 Plainchant

Monastic life in a community founded on relatively austere lines was no pushover in the 1940s. What could be seen to be sensible, reasonable requests by an individual monk could be met with a negative response, should the Novice Master, Prior or Abbot feel that that such requests could detract from an authentic, vowed Benedictine vocation. Sebastian encountered this early on when he recognised there was a space for a musician in the community and that this would require him time to practice. So far, so reasonable. However, the Novice Master, not himself a musician, only gave the young new arrival permission to practise for one hour a week! 'Little wonder' said Sebastian, 'that I had not made any progress'. However, a year after Dom Sebastian's ordination as a priest[30] in 1955, he was permitted to continue his study of music under the tutelage of the organist of Exeter Cathedral, Reginald Moore.

Moore, of whom Sebastian speaks warmly and with no small admiration, was born in Bramley, Leeds. He was a pupil of Sir Edward Bairstow and

---

[30] The Benedictine monastery, then as now, typically comprises ordained and non-ordained monks.

held several appointments as organist in and around Leeds before becoming assistant at **Salisbury Cathedral** in 1933. During the Second World War he served in the **Royal Air Force**. From 1947 to 1952 he was assistant music master at **Winchester College**.

Fig. 20 Dom Sebastian at his post

[Courtesy: Sebastian Wolff / Buckfast Abbey]

Sebastian studied under Moore, who he describes with characteristic kindness as 'a very good teacher', for some three and a half years after which he qualified for the prestigious Associateship of the Royal College of Organists. Whereas for many this would appear a tremendous step to have been reached, albeit on a journey forward in organ scholarship, instead, the erstwhile Novice Master and, now, Abbot, Dom Placid, directed Sebastian to forego further studies as he had 'done enough'. Sebastian could not countenance this; the rebel with a cause was set to complete his work with the Royal College and achieve the coveted Fellowship. This would take nothing short of four hours at night – every night – from 10pm to 2am after doing a day's work and with an early start beckoning.

This considerable sacrifice eventually paid off and, on 26th January 1963, Fr Sebastian was admitted a Fellow of the Royal College of Organists. A glance at the modern-day criteria for Fellowship is instructive:

Fellowship of the College indicates a standard of professional expertise in organ playing technique, advanced keyboard skills, and interpretative understanding, which at this level will be stylistically well informed. It also indicates accuracy in advanced aural perception, and accomplishment in those written disciplines (advanced stylistic techniques and analysis of performance and historical issues in relation to organ repertoire and its broader musical context) which support practical musicianship. [31]

---

[31] Criteria for modern-day Fellowship Diploma
https://www.rco.org.uk/pdfs/ExamRegulations17-18.pdf#page=15 viewed 5/4/2017

Anyone who has ever undertaken a course of part-time study will immediately recognise the self-discipline and resilience necessary, just to keep going and not to begin to resent that which one once loved. True, Sebastian was not troubled by domestic duties facing a family man or woman, but equally he was not supported by those words of encouragement that others might enjoy. What we have nowadays come to know as *emotional intelligence*, and those insights offered in the myriad of books that teach us how to get the best out of people, was, to put it mildly, not a major feature of pre-Vatican II religious life. The life grew toughness and was not without its many blessings, even if, in retrospect, it could, on occasion, be seen to lack humanity, on occasion.

At this time, Sebastian's music was, and very much remained, influenced by J.S. Bach. Indeed to have ever known him is to be acutely aware of his profound love and respect for this genius. This love came directly from Buckfast as it was here that Sebastian first encountered a powerful rendering of the work of the genius of Eisenach, through the good offices of Fr Gregory Burke OSB, organist of the Abbey.

Bach's compositional legacy includes examples in all major genres of the time except opera: nearly two hundred church cantatas; approximately two dozen secular cantatas; a handful of motets; the B-minor Mass and some shorter works with Latin texts; the *St. Matthew* and *St. John Passions*; the *Christmas*, *Easter*, and *Ascension Oratorios*; a large body of organ music (both free and based on chorales); many other important harpsichord works (e.g., Two- and Three-Part Inventions, *English* and *French Suites, Well-Tempered Clavier, Italian Concerto, Goldberg Variations*); chamber music; concertos (including the popular Brandenburg Concertos); the *Musical Offering;* and *The Art of Fugue.* Several of Bach's contemporaries were equally or even more prolific, but the uniformly high quality of his output is unparalleled.[32]

- [32] **Crist, S. [2011] Oxford Bibliographies** DOI: 10.1093/OBO/9780199757824-0043

The call of obedience

Again, the Hollywood movie might now see Fr Sebastian consolidating his well-deserved success with further musical achievements. However, the Hollywood director does not live the monastic life where obedience to the Abbot is intrinsic to the life. Just days later Sebastian received his marching orders: he was off to become, for a short time at least, an army chaplain at the home of the British army, Aldershot.

On arrival, briefed on his duties, he soon put his musical expertise to good use, playing for a wedding at St Michael's Garrison Church

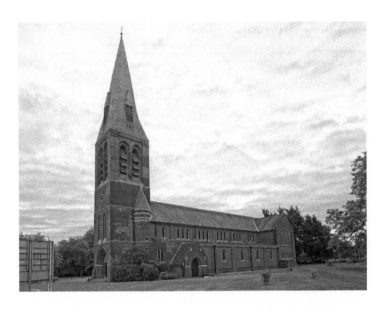

Fig. 21 The Garrison church of St Michael and St George, Aldershot

Posted to Salisbury plain, Sebastian's military career looked to take him next to a posting in Germany where, of course, his linguistic skills would have been invaluable, but this was not to be. The Medical Officer saw fit not to pass-as-fit the young Benedictine and, rather than boarding a plane to

Germany, Sebastian boarded a train to South Devon where, seamlessly and in a spirit of acceptance, he continued his normal monastic duties.

However, it was not long before the local Bishop came calling to ask Sebastian to become musical advisor to the Diocese of Plymouth. The timing was significant as the Second Vatican Council had just come to an end – a council whose impact on religious life and music would be significant and, for which, regarding the latter, Sebastain would offer his gifts as well as his, often trenchant, critique.

Fig. 22 While never 'off duty' monastic life had its 'down time' – young monks, both in and out of habit - relax in and around Dartmoor [Sebastian Wolff collection]

Chapter Five - The Second Vatican Council: Monastic life and Music

Fig. 23 Parish ministry – Dom Sebastian's parish ministry: a counterpoint to his music [Sebastian Wolff colllection]

The Second Vatican Council, the 21st ecumenical Council of the Roman Catholic Church (1962–

65), was announced by Pope Saint John XXIII on January 25, 1959, as a means of spiritual renewal for the Church. The work of the Council continued under Pope Saint John's successor, Pope [now Saint-] Paul VI, until the work of the Council was completed on December 8, 1965. Sixteen documents were enacted by the Council fathers.

The "Dogmatic Constitution on the Church" reflects the attempt of the Council Fathers to utilize biblical terms to describe the Church. The treatment of the hierarchical structure of the Church moves away from the tone of the first Vatican Council's teaching on the papacy by giving weight to the role of the bishops. The teaching of the constitution on the nature of the laity provided the basis for lay people to more clearly recognise their specific call to holiness, as well as recognise the Church not as static but as missionary. In describing the Church as a pilgrim people, the council fathers provided the theological justification for changing the defensive and inflexible stance that many, though not all, suggested had characterized much of Catholic thought and practice since the Protestant Reformation. This 'pilgrim people' required music to enhance their liturgical experience and, perhaps, unsurprisingly, this opened up the possibility of 'contemporary' [folk, pop...] music being used for the first time in mainstream liturgies. The issue for Sebastian, whatever the style, would always be one thing. Quality. 'People deserve decent music' he would say, often, it must be said, by way of lament.

The "Dogmatic Constitution on Divine Revelation" attempts to relate the role of Scripture and tradition to their common origin in the Word of

God that has been committed to the Church. The document affirms the value of Scripture for the salvation of men while maintaining an open attitude toward the scholarly study of the Bible. Here too there would be an opportunity for vernacular hymns and Mass settings to tap into scripture in a way that could be described, depending on one's point of view, as 'innovative and contemporary' or 'downright Protestant'.

The "Constitution on the Sacred Liturgy" established the principle of greater participation by the laity in the celebration of Mass and authorised significant changes in the texts, forms, and language used in the celebration of Mass and the administration of the sacraments. This would be highly significant for Sebastian and his musical contemporaries with the need for new music which engaged the congregation.

Finally, the "Pastoral Constitution on the Church in the World of Today" acknowledges the profound changes humanity is experiencing and attempts to relate the Church's concept of itself and of revelation to the needs and values of contemporary culture.

The Council also promulgated decrees (documents on practical questions) on the pastoral duties of bishops, ecumenism, the Eastern-rite Churches, the ministry and life of priests, the education for the priesthood, the religious life, the missionary activity of the Church, the apostolate of the laity, and the media of social communication. The impact on monastic life, including that at Buckfast, would be profound, not least in leading to the removal of the longstanding distinctions between [ordained] Choir Monks and [not ordained] 'Lay Brothers' such as the esteemed Brother Adam himself.[33]

Furthermore, declarations (documents on particular issues) on religious freedom, the Church's attitude toward non-Christian religions, and on Christian education were produced. These documents reflected the renewal in various areas of Church life begun decades before Pope Saint John—biblical, ecumenical, liturgical, lay apostolate. The impulse of the documents and the Council deliberations in general had, by the early 1970s. been felt in nearly every area of Church life

---

[33] These distinctions were no mere academic matter – the Lay Brothers lived separately and were explicitly 'other than' their ordained confreres. Whilst an emancipation for many Lay Brothers, Brother Adam valued his particular 'status' and identity, however old-fashioned that might seem.

and had set in motion many changes that may not have been foreseen by the Council Fathers.

The rebel in Sebastian found another legitimate outlet as the impact of the Second Vatican Council began to be felt throughout the Church. Dissatisfied though he was with his initial attempts to write in the vernacular for congregations, it was his horror at listening to some of the early responsorial psalms[34] that were being produced commercially that led him to write his own offerings – as much in protest as in creativity. Often characterising them as little more than 'pretty ditties', and while Sebastian's criticisms would not be shared by the

---

[34] The Psalms are the songs of the Church and the Responsorial Psalm is a song – often spoken but properly sung- embedded at the heart of the Liturgy of the Word in the eucharist.

entirety of the Catholic community, what was never in doubt was his motivation for making such trenchant remarks. 'People deserve better than this' he often said and, notwithstanding the fact that he would consistently find it an uphill struggle to replace what one might generously call 'accessible congregational music' with his own, he remained true to his convictions throughout. Little wonder then that he spent many years as the musical advisor to the Bishop of Plymouth, a role which took him to the highways and byways of Devon, Cornwall and Dorset.

Never one to eschew the challenge of more complex pieces and driven, as we have seen, by a belief that this post-conciliar *pilgrim* people should experience the musical equivalent of fine dining as against fast food, it was on the advice of a member of the Panel of Monastic Musicians that Sebastian set about writing a polyphonic setting of the Mass with organ accompaniment. The piece was duly completed and to Sebastian's pleasure, was the setting for a Mass celebrated in the Abbey Church by the late Cardinal Basil Hume, himself a Benedictine monk of Ampleforth. Supported by the choir of the former Buckfast Abbey school[35]and under the redoubtable baton of the School Choir Master, Trevor Jarvis, the piece was well received, though Sebastian later criticised himself for employing the vernacular. In a turn of fate which adds mystique, as well as inconvenience, the score was subsequently lost, surely to be discovered one day as a *Missam Amisa*. 'No doubt it will be found under a pile of music one day' said Sebastian, relaxed at the prospect.

---

[35] From 1967 until 1994, the Abbey ran a **prep school for boys aged 7-13**

Fully respecting the genius of the likes of Purcell, G.F. Handel and Vaughan Williams, Sebastian more and more saw in Latin – a musical language – the opportunity to write music which really offered the congregation a means of transcendence without the jagged edges of vernacular offerings. In addition, the idea that divine worship in the vernacular began with the Second Vatican Council is misleading, especially if one goes outside of the tradition whether to Lutheran pieces or, indeed, Tudor music. But within the Catholic Church a long tradition of adapting local songs and rhymes to the vernacular to spread religious messages had proved successful for Franciscans in mediaeval Europe[36] and, as early as the

---

[36] Alberts, Tara [2013:137] in *The Ashgate Research Companion to the Counter Reformation* [Eds. Alexandra Bamji, Geert H. Janssen and Mary Laven] London & New York: Routledge

1550s, for the Jesuits. Jettisoning any remaining reticence about the use of the vernacular at a time when the prelates of Trent[37] were urging the abandonment of the secular in liturgy, the Jesuits saw the use of the vernacular as critically important. Da Nobrega's Jesuit mission to Brazil, for instance, had 'arranged for the Our Father, the Ten Commandments and other prayers to be translated into the native Tupi and set to native-style tunes…a practice subsequently emulated in Mexico in the 1570s using the native Nahuarl.'[38]

---

[37] The Council of Trent, held between 1545 and 1563 in Trento (Trent) and Bologna, northern Italy, was one of the Roman Catholic Church's most important ecumenical councils. Prompted by the Protestant Reformation, it has been described as the embodiment of the Counter-Reformation.

[38] Monson, Craig [2006:417] in [Ed. James Haar] *European Music 1520-1640* Woodbridge: The Boydell Press

Importantly, Sebastian's love of music was a love he embraced *in the spirit* of the Second Vatican Council, not as some kind of protest or [neo-] conservative badge of honour. Offering it was, to him, a recognition of the dignity of the worshipping, pilgrim people of God to which so much of the Council was geared.

Fig. 24 Dom Sebastian celebrating the sacrament of baptism in the Abbey church. The Catholic notion of the sacrament as the outward sign of inner grace resonates with the sacramental of sacred music and reflects how the vocation of the ordained monastic musician is, authentically, the vocation of the priest-monk [Buckfast Abbey]

Chapter Six – Ministry

As a young man first encountering Dom Sebastian in the 1980s, what was immediately recognisable to this author was his ability with people. Whether firing off a cheery wave to, well, just about anyone, or in the more reflective moments of a one to one conversation, he had an uncanny ability to *be present* to the other person. This, coupled with a genuine interest in other people's lives and openness to what one might call life's existential messiness, he was sought after by many who needed a confessor, a spiritual director or just a quiet word. One of the many fans is local Farm Centre entrepreneur, Dr Chris Murray who, since his childhood, has had, what he terms, *the privilege of counting Fr Seb a friend.*

'Meeting Father Sebastian at fourteen was an eye opener having never met a monk nor priest before. Sebastian was accompanying Abbot Leo Smith on a social visit to a friend's house for afternoon tea . His kind personality shone, he was happy to discuss any topic, he wasn't 'religious' or ' pious' which made him very approachable for a teenager not bought up within a church-going home.'

Sebastian's ability to appear to the young Chris Murray as *not religious* was, of course, his ability to be approachable notwithstanding that his whole life could not have been more religious. But his generosity as a pastoral priest was significant and never to be underestimated as Chris Murray illustrates.

'I recall him coming to buy Christmas food hampers to give to parishioners he knew needed a treat and to experience the love of God in action.

On other occasions Sebastian shows how aware he is of those who need a lift – a break from life's hardships. He might approach us at Pennywell [farm centre] and ask for a ticket for someone who would benefit from a day out. Poor or rich, Catholic or not, Sebastian would do his best for someone else instinctively.'

Long before ecumenism took on the role it does today where there is, at least, a working assumption of good relationships between Christian churches of varying denominations, Sebastian had realised – whether through theological reflection, an instinctive missionary pragmatism or just a sense that you treat people the way you yourself would like to be treated- that he should form good relationships with his fellow clergy. This he duly did and his inter-Church Easter walks, co-celebrated interdenominational marriage blessings and the simple warmth he engendered among Anglicans, Methodists and the rest were the reason that any car journey into the local towns would see Sebastian offering a cheery salute to the full cross-section of Devon life.

'When I was a student Sebastian invited me to join him at Ashburton Methodist Church where they were raising funds for the church. He often would give free organ recitals as fund-raisers for any Christian denomination. It was a packed church and afterwards he invited myself and two other member so of the community out to the pub . We had a very jolly evening full of banter and jokes. it was the first time I discovered that monks and priests not only had a great sense of humour but were also great company.'

The experience of growing up in rural Ireland – of German parentage – as *the other* – was surely a strength for the older pastoral minister where charm, a listening ear and an absolute respect for the person he is addressing is much more effective than the bombast of those who might stand on their own apparent credentials and status.

Sebastian's warmth is instinctive but its efficacy to break down barriers to reveal the possibility of the divine is sacramental. Sebastian's power as an evangelist comes from his ability not to drive away the nervous or the cynical with speeches, jargon or guilt trips. Chris Murray continues:

> When I was a student we would sometimes go out for a drink and talk about 'God'. Sebastian was never pushy in evangelism and always happy to talk on any subject or talk about any situation, giving good counsel or scriptural example in answering a question. Deciding in my early twenties

that I was too much of a 'sinner' to either be a Christian or meet up with Father Seb we didn't meet for at least three years. We literally bumped into each other after I graduated and in my first job as an assistant farm manager I was draying some hay and, in a tight Devon lane, we met... just managed to stop in time! He leapt out of the car and said 'Christopher how lovely to see you, haven't seen you for so long' I realized that I hadn't been in contact as I was no longer interested in church, faith etc...I didn't tell him then that I felt too much a sinner to even go into a church! I just jokingly said I didn't believe in what he believed in so it would be a waste of time his spending time with me. His response was awesome.. "Do you drink!?' I replied in the affirmative so he then invited me to go for a drink...after

142

a beer or two and sharing with Sebastian 'where I was' in life he made me realise that being a sinner didn't bar me from either meeting him or going into a church. It was from this meeting that Father Seb gently 'brought me back into the fold.'

Fig 25. Fr Sebastian, Chris and Nicky Murray enjoy some table fellowship [Sebastian Wolff collection]

As the monastic organist and leading musician in the community, Sebastian has long benefitted from a modest studio from which he has composed extensively. But together with the fugues and the toccatas, the studio also offered many a visitor a place of hospitality, warmth and genuine care, consistent with the Benedictine apostolate of welcome. Chris Murray takes up a story of the legendary 'Sebastian's Den':

'It was always a treat to be invited to Sebastian's den for some post-Mass fellowship. Father Seb has, and always had, a great sense of deprecating humour which is always appreciated and goes well with all-comers, especially those who might buy into the stereotypes and caricatures of 'religious people'.

Chris also recalls how Sebastian's passion for music has never been, for him, a private or introspective faculty but, instead, something that should be shared for the benefit of all – and not only those within the precincts of the Abbey Church.

'Sebastian also used to teach music at Stoodley Knowle Convent School and is still very fondly remembered by the sisters and the girls; he has this amazing ability to reach out, befriend and support all people whoever they are. He also, famously, played at our wedding and played a celebration processional he had written himself. It was fantastic as the Landscove village church organ had never been given such exercise...the dust, mice , cobwebs and spiders were blasted out of every organ pipe as he gave the organ the full vent of what he'd written!'

But music was not the only creative outlet and, with a love of nature that would give St Francis a run for his money [if he had ever had any], Chris picks up on Sebastian's green fingers.

'The South Brent church [a church served by Buckfast] was the best place to hold the parish barbecue as the garden was superb. Father Seb loved his garden and planted out a fantastic array of flowers. He went to great lengths to make the church a welcoming place. When repainting the interior of the church he always ensured such activities were fun and accompanied by some good fuel…tonic wine and other delightful beverages. In his generosity he would often take people out for supper at a local hostelry which was another wonderful way he engaged with both his parishoners but also anyone and everyone especially if he saw they needed a bit of a 'lift' in life!'

Fig. 26 The refectory at Buckfast [Buckfast Abbey]

Of course a truly experienced pastoral priest must 'call it right' in a wide range of circumstances, some extremely distressing as Chris recalls"

'Father Sebastian was asked to say prayers at the crematorium on the tragic death of a lovely young man who used to repair our vehicles and tractors, who had been killed while riding his motorbike home back to Princetown from Buckfastleigh. He was just 30 years old. Sebastian asked me to accompany him to Exeter Cathedral where we met 250 plus mourners - many of them bikers with the corresponding taste in music. Amid the blaring of heavy metal music and the cold formality of the service Father Seb committed Dave's body to the flames with a prayerful sincerity that transcended age, class or religious conviction. A moment of sublime calm was captured - a godsend moment - bringing a quite secular and, on the face of it, quite daunting congregation, to God. The family were enormously comforted.

Somewhat less distressing but, for a young Chris Murray, of some import, was Sebastian's advice as to who Chris should ultimately marry. Whereas in some traditions of spiritual counselling the onus would have been entirely on the 'discerner' to reflect on how God was calling them, Sebastian used his instinct for people to grasp exactly Chris's character and drive and offer him the right advice. As Chris says: 'Thirty-five years on it was still the right call'.

When one speaks of healing in the context of priestly ministry, one may think of TV evangelists or the mystic powers of a St Pio [erstwhile Padre Pio]. However, Chris recalls Sebastian's own involvement in healing:

'Father Sebastian is a great man of prayer and care; several times he has personally asked me to pray for specific people in dire need or straights especially where health is concerned. On that point it was in the Abbey that I saw Father Sebastian anoint somebody and they sprang to life!!

During the Sunday Mass a chap collapsed; he was out as though dead. People called for a doctor and there was mild panic.

Father Sebastian was at the back of the Abbey having returned from saying Mass at Ashburton. He went straight over to the man, asked everyone to step back and anointed him. No sooner had he finished anointing the chap, he sprung to life; standing up he walked out of the Abbey and joined Sebastian and myself for coffee afterwards in the Abbey restaurant!'

Sebastian's popularity, without the aid of a *spin doctor*, purple prose or any Hollywood 'standout' event in his long ministry, could be seen as unusual. After all, Devon is hardly a strong Catholic part of the UK and the UK's secularism is well known. Monks and religious can be the subject of some suspicion – as they have been in this country for centuries – and there could be fair and unfair criticism that Sebastian's choice of life, however ascetic in its vows, has yet offered a certain comfort and security that many would desire in challenging and unpredictable times. So what is it that renders him capable of instinctively *calling the situation right?* Something surely to do with authenticity – being true to himself, his weaknesses as much as his strengths. But also it is his recognition of the extent to which the *sheep are scattered* that renders him the good shepherd he is. As Pope Francis said in a document that employs the word 'attractive' no less than sixteen times:

'We need to be realistic and not assume that our audience understands the full background to what we are saying, or is capable of relating what we say to the very heart of the Gospel which gives it meaning, beauty and attractiveness.'

[Evangelii Gaudium – The Joy of the Gospel [2013:34]

Of course, this is also the modality of the missionary. In 1990, Pope John Paul II issued his massive encyclical on the "permanent validity of the Church's missionary mandate," [*Redemptoris Missio*]. Perhaps the most significant section for the theme of this chapter is found in Chapter 2, a chapter that focuses on "The Kingdom of God." The Church's task, rather than focusing on its own extension, exists to announce and inaugurate God's reign among all peoples. The Church's existence is not for itself; it exists for another reason: to be the sacrament of God's presence already revealed in Christ, and to continue Christ's mission of preaching, serving, and witnessing to the eschato-logical fullness of that presence in history. The Church does not properly, therefore, have a mission. The mission—God's mission of redeeming, healing, loving the world—has a Church to serve it. Or again, from *Evangelii Gauudium:* 'that missionary outreach is paradigmatic for all the Church's activity' [15].

While the specific vocation of the monastic differs from that of the mendicant and apostolic orders [such as the Franciscans, Jesuits] the opportunity within the English Benedictine Congregation for fully-fledged apostolic endeavour has long been a proud tradition and it is in this context that Sebastian, in his own way, took hold of the missionary mandate.

However the missionary mandate, apostolic zeal and love for the flock exist within a temporality which catches up on all of us and the time came for Sebastian to finally retire from his formal, pastoral post. Chris Murray recalls:

'When Sebastian was retired from the parish, showing the love and regard in which he is held, the parishioners arranged a lunch in South Brent village hall. It was packed with his flock and more! Gifts were given, eulogies said and everyone wanted him to know how much he was appreciated, how much he was loved and how much they would miss him. He was a brilliant parish priest and made enormous strides to visit homes, encourage all and engage with the wider village community.'

Fig. 27 A word for every occasion

[Sebastian Wolff collection]

Chapter Seven - A brief commentary on the organ music of Sebastian and a list of his choral music - By Dr A. H. Claire

The writer wishes to acknowledge the following for their invaluable assistance with this article. Fr Sebastian himself, for his friendship and many hours of conversation (and not just about music). Jennifer Bate, Sr Margaret Truran and Trevor Jarvis for their warm hearted (and witty) tributes.Jeremy Filsell for his excellent recording of some of Fr Sebastian's organ music. In fact this is the last recording of the Ralph Downes instrument, made in 1999.

The original organ was designed by Ralph Downes, and was in many ways the precursor to his more famous instruments in Brompton Oratory, Gloucester Cathedral and The Royal Festival Hall.

At the time, Downes' ideas were revolutionary, featuring low wind pressures and a 'baroque' style of voicing, being influenced by the 'classical' European organ then being 'rediscovered'. It could be seen as a reaction against the 'orchestral' 'town hall' type of organ that had developed over the previous centuries. So it's possible to see this essentially 'neo – classical' organ as an ideal inspiration to Fr. Sebastian's essentially 'neo classical' musical language – with a debt to the great J S Bach, the Lutheran Chorale, Mendelssohn and the more modern masters, including Flor Peeters, and the great French tradition, especially Messiaen and Langlais. Almost certainly one can hear also the English pastoralism of Vaughan Williams and also the Irish Celtic influence, particularly in his choral writing.

And maybe above all, the building itself, the Catholic 'mysticism', the timeless Gregorian Chant...

FANTASIA AND FUGUE

This is one of Fr Sebastian's most substantial organ pieces.

In his notes to his CD recording of this piece, Jeremy Filsell describes the Fantasia as a 'sonata-type movement'. Perhaps it is best seen as a true 'Fantasia' i.e. a somewhat improvisatory structure with the following 'ingredients'-

1. A 'fanfare' (with dotted rhythms),
2. A faster section based on a dotted melody accompanied by toccata figurations based on diminished chord harmony
3. A softer syncopated section using whole tone harmony
4. A short fanfare for 'trumpets'

5. Return of section 2 now expanded

6. More sustained, softer section played on 'flutes'

7. Return of section 1 'fanfare'

8. A sort of toccata-like 'coda'

The harmonic language throughout is amongst Fr Sebastian's most advanced, with particular use of parallel fourths, diminished and whole-tone harmonies. The fugue, by contrast, uses a more conservative harmonic idiom, which Filsell says 'perhaps acknowledges a Mendelssohnian debt'. The Fugue's main subject is based on the opening 'Fanfare' of the preceding Fantasia. It has two (fairly) regular countersubjects and builds to a grand finish.

INTRODUCTION, CHORALE and **FUGUE** 'Let all Mortal Flesh Keep Silent'

The Introduction is dedicated 'For Fr James Courtney O.S.B., Buckfast Abbey', and is marked *Adagio*, It is a florid 'overture-type' movement in the baroque style. The Chorale is a slow meditation with the melody in the tenor. The Fugue, marked *Allegro moderato*, is based on the melody throughout with a hint of the florid 'baroque' writing returning towards the end.

The melody of 'Let all mortal flesh', known as *Picardy*, dates back to the 17th Century, and was originally used for the folk song "*Jesus-Christ s'habille en pauvre*". It was popularised when incorporated by Vaughan Williams into the English Hymnal (1906). It is a beautiful melody in the Dorian mode.

AURORA LUCIS RUTILAT

(Easter Chorale). This is based on an Easter Hymn, sometimes attributed to St. Ambrose

Auróra lucis rútilat,
cælum resútat láudibus,
mundus exsúltans iúbilat,
gemens inférnus úlulat.

Dawn reddens with light,
the sky resounds with praise,
the exulting world rejoices,
the weeping netherworld wails,

This setting is delightfully pastoral in mood, with the melody appearing in the tenor, accompanied by a lilting accompaniment.

CHORALE PRELUDE ON ADORO TE

Dedicated 'To my friend Michael Scoble', this is a meditative setting of the Eucharistic Hymn, *A-doro te Devote*, by Thomas Aquinas. The Gerard Manley Hopkins translation is well known –

Godhead here in hiding, whom I do adore,

Masked by these bare shadows, shape and nothing more,

See, Lord, at thy service low lies here a heart

Lost, all lost in wonder at the God thou art.

The melody appears in the soprano part, accompanied by mellifluous (though sometimes highly chromatic) counterpoint.

CHRISTE REDEMPTOR (Hymn for Vespers of Christmas)

Christmas Chorale Prelude for Organ (Plainsong hymn for the 1st Vespers of Christmas).

This setting alternates a florid melody for flute stops with a 4-part harmonisation of the melody, chorale style, on the string stops.

Christe Redemptor omnium,
Ex Patre Patris Unice,
Solus ante principium
Natus ineffabiliter:

O Christ, redeemer of all people,
The Father's only Son,
Only you, before all rulers,
Ineffably were born of the Father

CARILLON (Homage to Mulet & Vierne)

Composed for the Blessing of Rt Rev David Charlesworth, Abbot of Buckfast

25 February 1992

This is a virtuoso composition, full of exuberance and *élan*. As suggested in the subtitle, it reflects the French tradition of *Carillons* i.e. pieces suggesting the pealing of bells, usually by a repetitive toccata texture – the famous examples being Louis Vierne's *Carillon de Westminster* and Henri Mulet's *Carillon Sortie*, both in D major, as is this piece. This piece exists in an even more extrovert version for two trumpets and organ.

Organ Music, Volume 2, for Lent and Easter [1994]

Chorale: O Sacred Head

Fanfare for Easter Day

Entry for Easter Sunday Morning [based on Easter Hymn]

Chorale: At the Lamb's High feast

Chorale Partita: Christ the Lord is Risen Again (Orientis Partibus) 'To my friend, David Precious'

The Chorale **O SACRED HEAD** is a setting of the well-known Passion Chorale melody, *Herzlich tut mich verlangen*, originally by Hans Leo Hassler and adapted by Johann Crüger. Bach famously harmonised versions in his St Matthew Passion. The most familiar English translation is by Robert Bridges -

O Sacred Head, sore wounded,
Defiled and put to scorn;

O kingly head, surrounded
With mocking crown of thorn:
What sorrow mars Thy grandeur?
Can death Thy bloom deflow'r?
O countenance whose splendour
The hosts of heav'en adore!

This setting, marked *Lento*, consists of the melody, with minimal ornamentation accompanied by gently repeated chords, moving stepwise in pairs (*appoggiatura*s), a well-known baroque *affekt*, suggesting 'weeping'. The texture is reminiscent of the chorale prelude attributed to Bach, 'Erbarme dich mein, O Herre Gott' BWV721

The **FANFARE FOR EASTER DAY**, marked 'With dignity' is a joyful paean, suggesting the pealing of bells and containing some dramatic modulations.

The **ENTRY FOR EASTER SUNDAY MORNING**, again marked 'With dignity' is based on the well-known 'Easter Hymn', the melody from *Lyra Davidica* (1708) and sung to the words 'Jesus Christ is Risen Today'. The melody appears in the pedals.

Jesus Christ is ris'n today, Alleluia!
our triumphant holy day, Alleluia!
who did once upon the cross, Alleluia!
suffer to redeem our loss. Alleluia!

AT THE LAMB'S HIGH FEAST is a trio – the slightly ornamented melody in the left hand (registration – trumpet + 2'), the right hand playing a sparkling counter melody, and the pedals providing a 'walking bass'. The melody, known as 'Salzburg' is from 1678 and by Jakob Hintze. The text is an English paraphrase of the Latin Hymn *Ad regias Agni dapes.*

At the Lamb's high feast we sing,
Praise to our victorious King,
Who hath washed us in the tide
Flowing from his piercèd side;
Praise we Him, Whose love divine
Gives His sacred blood for wine,
Gives His body for the feast,
Love the victim, love the priest.

CHRIST THE LORD IS RISEN AGAIN

(Orientis Partibus) – Chorale Partita is a suite of

variations on the 12th century Latin song, usually attributed to Pierre de Corbeil.

Firstly, we hear a straight forward 4-part harmonisation of the melody. The 1st variation is a two part setting (known as *bicinium*) – the ornamented melody accompanied by a florid left hand. Variation II is a mellifluous setting in 3 parts, the top part in triplets, the melody in the alto, and a lilting bass – reminiscent of Bach's 'Jesu, Joy of Man's desiring'. Variation III is a canon at the fifth between the soprano and bass parts, the left hand providing a severe accompaniment using parallel 4ths. Variation IV is a *toccata-carillon* type setting with the melody played on the pedals. Variation V (Fugue) is in 4 parts complete with regular countersubject, *stretto* and a *fff* chordal peroration marked *organo pleno* (full organ) with the melody thundering in the pedals.

Organ Music, Volume 1, for Advent and Christ-mas [1997]

Advent Chorale

O Come Emmanuel

Lo! He Comes [also later set for voices and or-gan in 'Cantata for a New Era']

Unto us is born a Son (Partita) Dedicated to Jennifer Bate

Chorale Prelude on the Somerset Carol

ADVENT CHORALE is a setting in the style of Bach's Orgelbüchlein. The melody is known as Salisbury, and is from Thomas Ravenscroft's *The Whole Booke of Psalmes* (1621). The present writer has been unable to find the Advent text associated with this tune, and Fr Sebastian cannot recall the text either!

O COME EMMANUEL is quite a severe setting, using parallel 4ths, reminding the present writer of Hindemith. The melody is presented *ff* in the pedals. **LO! HE COMES WITH CLOUDS DESCENDING** is a setting of the familiar Advent melody, *Helmsley*.

Lo! He comes, with clouds descending, once for our salvation slain;

thousand thousand saints attending swell the triumph of His train.

Alleluia! Alleluia! Alleluia! God appears on earth to reign.

This setting alternates a florid baroque-style melody with a 4 part harmonisation of the melody phrase by phrase.

UNTO US IS BORN A SON (Partita) - Dedicated to Jennifer Bate.

Basically a theme and five variations begins with a 4-part harmonisation of the melody, in typical Wolff style – i.e. the part-writing causing gentle dissonances. Variation 1 is a *bicinium*, i.e. a 2-part setting with a florid bass. Variation 2 is a canon at the octave between the pedals an right hand, the left hand providing an undulating chromatic accompaniment.

Variation 3 is a *toccata-carillon* type setting, with the melody in the pedals. In Variation 4 the right

hand plays a slightly ornamented version of the melody (on a reed stop) with the accompaniment becoming quite chromatically discordant. Variation 5 is a *Fugato* that soon develops into *carillon* style textures.

CHORALE PRELUDE ON THE SOMERSET CAROL is a rather grandiose setting of this folk carol.

The carol was collected from a Mr. Rapsey, of Bridgwater by Cecil Sharp and first published in 1905. Rapsey said the carol had been taught to him by his mother and that, in company with other children, he used to sing it in the streets of Bridgwater at Christmas time, thus fitting it in with the *Wassail* tradition. The carol was later used by Sharp's friend and fellow collector, Ralph Vaughan

Williams, in his 1912 Fantasia on Christmas Carols.

Come all you worthy gentlemen
That may be standing by.
Christ our blessed Saviour
Was born on Christmas day.
The blessed virgin Mary
Unto the Lord did say,
O we wish you the comfort and tidings of joy!

Organ Music, Volume 3, for Various Occasions

Come Holy Ghost

Most Ancient of all Mysteries: Prelude

Chorale for Feasts of the B.V.M. and Epiphany

Chorale on a melody by Orlando Gibbons

Nocturne

Our Father

Processional March

COME HOLY GHOST is based on the well-known melody *Tallis' Ordinal*, the English words being a translation of *Veni, Creator Spiritus*. It is composed in a strict baroque chorale-prelude style, whereas each phrase of the melody (played in the pedals) is preceded by imitative counterpoint based on the phrase's notes in diminution.

Come, Holy Ghost, Creator, come
From thy bright heav'nly throne,
Come take possession of our souls,
And make them all thy own.

MOST ANCIENT OF ALL MYSTERIES is a setting of the melody St. Flavian, the text by F. W. Faber.

Most ancient of all mysteries,

Before Thy throne we lie;

Have mercy now, most merciful,

Most holy Trinity.

A flowing setting with the melody in the tenor, containing some delightful harmonic 'twists'.

CHORALE FOR FEASTS OF THE B.V.M. AND EPIPHANY is an Adagio and Fugue based on the melody *Liebster Immanuel* and dedicated to Raymond and Fiona McCluskey. Usually sung to the words –

Brightest and best of the stars of the morning,
Dawn on our darkness, and lend us thine aid;
Star of the East, the horizon adorning,
Guide where our infant Redeemer is laid.

The *Adagio* is a florid setting in the minor mode, although the melody itself is usually harmonised in the major mode. The Fugue follows, *Allegro Moderato*.

CHORALE ON A MELODY BY ORLANDO GIBBONS is a setting of Song 1, often sung to the words 'Thou, who at thy first Eucharist didst pray'. This setting reminds the present writer of Vaughan Williams *Rhosymedre*, also in G major.

Thou, who at Thy first Eucharist didst pray
That all Thy Church might be forever one,

Grant us at every Eucharist to say
With longing heart and soul, Thy will be done.
O may we all one bread, one body be,
Through this blest sacrament of unity.

The **NOCTURNE** (dedicated to Trevor Jarvis) is a dreamy Adagio.

OUR FATHER is a setting of the Lutheran melody *Vater unser im Himmelreich*, marked *Allegro moderato*, and featuring throughout a 'rolling' triplet texture.

PROCESSIONAL was composed for the wedding of Fr Sebastian's sister.

It is unashamedly in the Parry/Elgar/Walton tradition complete with a central section *nobilmente* melody.

FOR A FESTIVE OCCASION- For Elizabeth Keane

Elizabeth Keane is the organist at St Brendan's Cathedral, Loughrea, Co. Galway, Ireland, the very Cathedral where Sebastian's father was organist. This Fanfare-style piece relies a lot on discordant harmonies based on parallel 4ths and 5ths and suggests the clashing of bells with timpani – like punctuations in the pedals.

TE BEATA SPONSA CHRISTI [2004] - Dedicated to Dame Margaret Truran, O.S.B.[39]

---

[39] Sr. Margaret Truran was a pianist and violist before entering the monastery and was for many years, organist and teacher of the choir of the Abbey of Stanbrook, England. She has given public lectures and written articles on the liturgy, especially on Gregorian chant and on liturgical theology.

Te beata sponsa Christi,

Te, columba virginum,

Siderum tollunt coloni

Laudibus, Scholastica:

Nostra te lætis salutant

Vocibus præcordia.

Ye blessed spouse of Christ! O Dove of the cloister! The citizens of heaven proclaim thy merits, and we, too, sing Scholastica's praises with joyful hymns and loving hearts.

This setting is vintage Wolff i.e. immaculate mellifluous counterpoint accompanying the melody in the tenor.

A LIST OF CHORAL COMPOSITIONS BY SEBASTIAN WOLFF

Requiem

This work is dedicated to all those who have died as a consequence of war, particularly in this century. Also to the memory of my parents, deceased monks of Buckfast, and my departed friends, especially Hugh McCluskey, Bema Bass-Twitchell and Susan Frost.

Buckfast Abbey 1991

Requiem aeternam – Kyrie Eleison – Sanctus – Benedictus – Pie Jesu – Agnus Dei – Libera Me – In paradisum

Responsorial Psalms and Gospel Acclamations – Year A 1992

Responsorial Psalms & Gospel Acclamations Year B 1993

Responsorial Psalms and Gospel Acclamations Year C (1993)

Buckfast Mass [1994]

Penitential Rite – Gloria – Sanctus – Great Amen – Agnus Dei

Westminster Festival Mass [1995]

For Congregation and Choir

With Fanfares for Holy Saturday

Lord have Mercy – Fanfare for Holy Saturday – Gloria – Sanctus – Great Amen – Lamb of God

Missa Brevis [1995]

In honour of Our Lady of Buckfast

Kyrie Eleison – Gloria – Sanctus – Benedictus
– Agnus Dei

Ave Maria – Motet for six voices

Dedicated to Martyn Warren and Voces as a token of gratitude for their services to the Abbey.

St Cecilias's Day 1997

Cantata for a New Era [1999] - Words arranged by Alison Gagg

The Dawn of Salvation

Introduction: In the beginning

Chorus: Let us make man in our own image and likeness

The Fall Organ introduction

Reading: The serpent was more subtle than any beast of the field which the Lord had made.

Chorus: Loss of trust returned to dust

Reading: So the Lord God expelled Adam

Hymn: thou whose almighty Word

Prophecy of Salvation

Recitative: The people that walked in darkness

Aria: Arise!, shine! Your light is come

Recitative; A virgin is with child

Reading: That day the Lord will start his threshing

Chorus: How beautiful on the mountains

Birth and Mission of John the Baptist

Reading: In the days of King Herod of Judaea

Recitative; An angel of the Lord appeared to Zechariah

Chorus: he will be great in the sight of the Lord

Duo: Listen to the voice

Chorale; Hush! the world is still and waiting

The Birth of the Saviour

Reading: Now at this time Caesar Augustus issued a decree

Recitative and Chorus: Shepherds guarding their flocks by night

Reading: Now when the angels had gone

Final Chorus: Rejoice, rejoice, let all men rejoice

Lullaby Carol (2004)

O Sacrum Convivium [2005] - As a token of appreciation to Martyn Warren and Voces

Missa Solemnis (in preparation)

Kyrie – Gloria – Sanctus – Agnus Dei

Plymouth Cathedral 150th Anniversary Mass

In honour of the Annunciation of the Blessed Virgin Mary

Lord Have Mercy – Glory to God – Holy, Holy, Holy – Great Amen – Lamb of God – Fanfare for Easter day

Christus Vincit

For Choir and Congregation (& trumpet)

Congregational Mass of St. Brendan

(Dedicated to Mgr. Cathal Geraghty and the assistant priests of St. Brendan's Cathedral, Loughrea)

Penitential Rite – Lord have mercy – Gloria – Sanctus – Great Amen – Agnus Dei

Chapter Eight - Fellow Travellers – voices of appreciation

A tribute to Dom Sebastian by Jennifer Bate

I played five concerts in Buckfast Abbey during the 1980s. On arrival the first time, in 1980, Dom Sebastian met me with a wonderful welcome. I asked to hear the organ from the body of the church and he launched into a spectacular improvisation which thoroughly demonstrated the instrument he knew and loved. I was absolutely thrilled, and he sensed my excitement. We were friends from that moment on.

The initial visit was part of the Dartington Summer School of Music. I was invited for two programmes: the first was with the Taverner Consort conducted by Andrew Parrott, where I accompanied the Messe de Notre Dame by Guillaume de Machaut and Liszt's Via Crucis, with these great pieces interspersed with some Bach solo pieces. The following night, my programme was entirely organ music by Messiaen. I gained the impression that my work with le Maître particularly fascinated Dom Sebastian.

Obviously, I had to stop rehearsing for services, but I always made a point of staying to listen to his magical, subtle accompaniments to the Gregorian chants. This is no easy task, for the music was not written to be accompanied in the first place; however, his gentle support to the singing was so sensitive, it was sure to move the heart of anyone sitting in the Abbey.

My return to Buckfast in 1982 was very special because it was part of the celebrations of the centenary of the Abbey. Together with Dom Sebastian, I designed a programme to reflect this. It included some of his favourite composers: Bach, Brahms, Ropek, Howells, Peeters, Messiaen and Langlais.

The 1983 concert was all French music and, again, part of the Dartington Summer School. The first half was organ music by Messiaen and then we performed the Fauré Requiem. I think that Dom Sebastian must have particularly enjoyed that occasion, because he then wrote a set of variations on Unto us a Son is born. I am very proud that it is dedicated "To my dear Friend Jennifer".

My last time (so far!) was as part of the Ashburton Festival, when I was able to give the premiere performance of the piece he wrote for me.

What do I remember most? Well, fun and laughter, relaxing after practising, and talking about music. We had marvellous conversations and, like a magician, he would produce bottles of 'the brew' (special quality!) that had been hidden in numerous secret pockets in his habit!

A Tribute from Sr Margaret Truran, OSB

In the late 1960s the choirmistress at Our Lady and St Neot, Liskeard, Cornwall, returned from a diocesan meeting at Buckfast bearing a draft setting of the Mass Ordinary by an unknown Dom

Sebastian Wolff. It stood out from the ditties being created to meet the dearth of music in the vernacular, and was to greet me again when I entered Stanbrook.

There I met Father Sebastian when he attended a meeting of monastic musicians. The young novice was sent to the organ loft during Mass to guide him through the idiosyncrasies of Stanbrook compositions, duplicated in fading blue ink. The occasional comments could evoke a surprising response. 'That piece without any indication is in the first mode, up a tone.' 'Ah yes. Do you have to listen to that drivel every day?' He was referring not to the singing but to the homily; our valiant chaplain was near the end of his life. The absence of humbug and dry humour made an unforgettable impression.

So did his courtesy towards young organists in the English Benedictine Congregation.

He would show us his organ compositions at meetings and offer copies to anyone who wanted them. The partita *Unto us is born a Son* has for nearly thirty years been heard during the Christmas season at Stanbrook and in Rome. The dedication (could there have been a twinkle in the composer's eye?) of the chorale prelude on the Gregorian hymn *Te beata sponsa Christi* (2004) ensures that it is played on the feast of St Scholastica and also when the same melody is sung at Michaelmas.

When Father Sebastian's three-year cycle of Responsorial Psalms for Sundays was published,

Stanbrook already had settings for virtually every day of the liturgical year. However, the threefold style of a response, psalm tone and meditative organ interlude is so effective that several compositions were incorporated into the repertoire. Among the favourites are Psalm 65, "Cry out with joy to God, all the earth", splendid for Eastertide; Psalm 83, "How lovely is your dwelling place"; and Psalm 95, "Proclaim the wonders of the Lord". The glorious setting of Psalm 106, "O give thanks to the Lord, for his love endures for ever," inspired the title of a joint recording by the monks of Prinknash and nuns of Stanbrook. The original was remastered for a CD, Chant and Psalms, that offers a continuing opportunity to hear Father Sebastian's little gem.

Elizabeth Keane

Director/Organist St. Brendan's Cathedral, Loughrea

As a seventeen-year old music student I first encountered Fr. Sebastian while I was practising organ in St. Brendan's Cathedral, Loughrea. Unaware of his musical talent we struck up a conversation about Loughrea and his connection with the place. Both families were from the town and were involved in the community. His warmth, kindness and wit led to a lifelong friendship and his encouragement, advice and guidance has influenced my musical   progression. Over a large glass of brandy one winter's evening he suggested that he write a piece of music for me reflecting my style and interests. Little did I realize that he would write such a piece considering his workload and commitments. I was truly humbled when it arrived in the post. I was even more delighted to hear about the publication of his biography. His story needs to be heard, his musical talent acknowledged by all and I'm proud, honoured and humbled to call him a true friend

Trevor Jarvis

I first encountered Fr Sebastian in September 1978, when I was appointed Director of Music at Buckfast Abbey School. As well as looking after music in the school, my brief also included the training of the choristers who sang in the Abbey Church three times a week. There was a School Mass at midday on Wednesdays, sung Benediction on Saturday evenings and the Conventual Mass on Sunday mornings. It was in the latter service that my work dovetailed with Fr Sebastian. At the time he was parish priest in South Brent, with a Mass there on Sunday mornings, after which he would drive back to take over the organ playing from myself in time for the Communion hymn [provided that he wasn't held up] and the outgoing voluntary. Normally he made it, although there were some (mercifully rare) instances when he didn't! I remember those occasions when I had to hastily rummage through my stack of organ music and find something that I could play 'off the cuff' at a moment's notice.

Fr Sebastian's lasting legacy will no doubt be his compositions, currently available only at Buckfast Abbey, and produced 'in house'. However, the best of his works deserve a wider circulation than this. A notable achievement was his composing the Responsorial Psalms for the entire three-year cycle, including all the various feast days of the Church's year, completed in 1991. This filled a void, and was a real labour of love. Inevitably, given the sheer number of Responses set, some worked better than others – but amongst this collection there are some gems. Other works written for choirs include The Requiem, written in 1994, a congregational Mass of St Brendan in a responsorial style, and the rather more festive Westminster Mass, for choir and congregation, with fanfares for Holy Saturday. More complex, and perhaps less memorable was his Centenary Mass. However, it is his organ compositions which stand out especially. Here, he shows complete mastery in writing of chorale preludes, fanfares, and particularly well-constructed fugues.

Fr Sebastian was ever ready to help me personally, even with the most prosaic tasks such as giving me a lift in his car to collect my cats from their boarding place in South Brent at the start of a new term. These car journeys were memorable in two ways. Firstly, driving through South Brent, where he was Parish Priest, involved much hand-waving salutes between him and various villagers, that one had the sensation of making a royal progress. Secondly, Fr Sebastian would spend the journey recounting a series of jokes and funny stories he had heard recently. As he delivered the punch-line, he would inevitably turn towards me to see if I had got the joke. As we were hurtling along the country lane between Buckfast and Brent at the time, my response, whilst staring intently through the windscreen, was somewhat rather strained.

Final thoughts

If Sebastian's life was a Hollywood movie he would have started at the foot of the mountain, climbed it, fallen off a couple of times and then finally reached the pinnacle. Or, perhaps more appropriately, using the metaphor of the fugue, his life would have begun with exposition, moved through development and returned to the subject's tonic key. But lives are rarely built this way. Instead, whether travelling through pastoral South Devon to serve a tiny congregation, composing a responsorial psalm, entertaining a guest in his legendary 'den' or providing common-sense guidance to a troubled soul, Sebastian epitomises that faculty of deriving the extraordinary from the ordinary. Or, to borrow from Jesuit spirituality, of finding God in all things.

Sebastian began his life surrounded in a blizzard of differing influences, some good and some very painful. German parents with high expectations and, on occasion, providing at best what we might, nowadays, call tough love. A rural Irish childhood, much promoted and vaunted by the politics of de Valera,[40] where the bucolic could mask a very real poverty. A wartime fear of, and prejudice towards, the migrant with all its contemporary resonances. A Catholic Church, triumphant, yet not always as kind as it could have been. It was into this soup, like all of us, that Sebastian was, in the words of an other famous German, *thrown*[41] . This book is warm, perhaps overly hagiographic, but the first

---

[40] Éamon de Valera [1882-1975] led his party Fianna Fáil to adopt policies based on his belief that the Catholic church and the family were central to Irish identity

[41] Martin Heidegger, *Being and Time* [1953:241]

person to cry No! to any attempt at depicting this as the life of a saint would be Sebastian himself. What Sebastian's life reminds those of us who have had the pleasure of sharing it is that the possibility for holiness subsists precisely in that messiness and pragmatism that makes life what it is. Any modern-day 360 degree *appraisal* of the strengths and weaknesses of Fr Sebastian would find plenty to say on all sides, as it would for us all, but this is precisely why his ministry has been efficacious. To our cry of 'I am not worthy' , Sebastian retorts, 'sit down and have a drink'. To our hubristic assertion that 'I have done the unforgivable', he reminds us of a God whose omnipotence would suggest otherwise and whose love would demand otherwise. Sebastian's 'theology' [though he would balk at the pretentiousness of this] is predicated on incarnation – the Word made flesh. Jesus encountering us *as we are* and not as our inner *Spin Doctor* might like to portray us. Not a Jesus of academic debate but rather the one who smiles at the sinner and draws figures, not in gold leaf, but in the very dust of the highways and byways on which we are all called to walk.

****

Beattie, G. [1997]. Beattie, Gordon [1997]. *Gregory's Angels: A history of the addyes, priories, parishes and schools of the monks and nuns following the Rule of St Benedict in Great Britain, Ireland and their overseas foundations : to commemorate the arrival of St Augustine in Kent in 597 AD* Hereford : Gracewing

Emery, A. [2006]. *Greater Medieval Houses of England and Wales, 1300-1500,* (Vol. Volume 3.). (n.d.). Cambridge: Cambridge University Press

Heidegger, M. [1953] *Being and Time* [trans. Stambaugh, J.] New York : State University of New York

Independent, The. (1995, December 28). Obituary: Abbot Placid Hooper

Stallworthy, J. [2013]. *Anthem for Doomed Youth: Twelve Soldier Poets of the First World War.* London : Constable & Robinson.

Time (1943, Aug 16)

205

9 783743 998810